EFFECTIVE
SPELLING

A *practical guide for teachers*

Norma Mudd

Hodder & Stoughton

A MEMBER OF THE HODDER HEADLINE GROUP

In association with the United Kingdom Reading Association

Cataloguing in Publication Data is available from the British Library

ISBN 0-340-58733-4

First published 1994
Impression number   10 9 8 7 6 5 4 3 2 1
Year   1998   1997   1996   1995   1994

Typeset by Rowland Phototypesetting Limited, Bury St Edmunds, Suffolk.
Printed in Great Britain for Hodder & Stoughton Educational, a division of
Hodder Headline Plc, 338 Euston Road, London NW1 3BH by St Edmundsbury
Press Ltd, Bury St Edmunds, Suffolk.

Contents

Preface

The teaching of spelling is a subject which is guaranteed to provoke differences of opinion among the population in general. There are those who will argue that time given to class spelling instruction is time wasted, since children need to be considered as individuals and either are, or are not, naturally good spellers. Others may refer back with nostalgia to the 'Good old days' when children were given daily spellings to learn which were subsequently tested each week.

It is the aim of this book to consider children as individuals who have different levels of spelling achievement *and* to give practical examples of how both infant and junior children may be helped to improve and extend their knowledge about spellings via regular, relevant and systematic instruction, so that the majority may embark upon writing tasks with confidence. Instruction and assessment are linked to the requirements of the National Curriculum. Moreover, the spelling instruction is described in relation to writing (and often reading), and not as an isolated, discrete subject. At times it may appear that some of the suggestions for spelling instruction are over-prescriptive, but I consider that for at least two decades, newly-trained teachers have suffered greatly (and, in turn, so have their children) from a lack of direction in this area. Frequently, student teachers have been advised merely that children should be encouraged to concentrate upon content rather than spelling.

Of course, the content is the most important aspect of any written work; and correctly spelled, neatly presented but banal writing is generally valueless – except to illustrate the writer's abilities in spelling and handwriting. Yet surely, we, as teachers, should encourage quality writing which is also spelled according to the best of the writer's ability. It has been my experience that if children are given instruction in spelling to suit their level of ability and interests from an early age, then quality work may be even more forthcoming, since they are often able to express themselves well and clearly due to their confidence in their spelling abilities.

Marie Clay's 'reading recovery programme' (1990) which has proved to be extremely successful (though expensive) in the United Kingdom as well as New Zealand, seeks to remedy and help children to 'recover' lost ground in reading. It thus seems logical to follow Clay's exhortation to provide early intervention and apply it to spelling so that positive attitudes may be promoted in children long before they label themselves as poor spellers and face writing tasks with dread. My experience in adult basic education (ABE) has indicated that the self-esteem of far too many adults is virtually at zero level, because they have not received appropriate help or instruction in spelling at an early stage in their learning. Chapter 9 is included to help teachers who have children with spelling difficulties.

In any subject, the most succesful teaching generally results from teachers who have an interest in their subject which they are able to pass on to their pupils. The teaching of spelling is no exception to this generalisation. In order to give teachers some background information on the origins and development of our language, Chapter 2 gives information regarding the many influences which have produced the language which we use today and which have resulted in our modern spellings. The chapter includes explanations of some of the irregular sound/symbol correspondences in our language which frequently cause difficulties for some novice spellers. Additionally, Chapter 8 includes some common examples of words and prefixes in our language which have their origins in Latin, French and Greek languages. Armed with this information, children may not only learn about spelling, but also be able to make educated guesses about word meanings.

If this book serves to promote thought, discussion and evaluation among teachers regarding the nature and quality of their writing and spelling instruction, then it will have achieved its aim.

Acknowledgements

My very special thanks are given to my daughter, Catherine, who gave me tremendous support throughout the writing of this book.

I should also like to thank Roger Beard, my editor, for his invaluable advice and help, and the friends, teachers and children (especially in Burscough County Primary School and Burscough Methodist School) who contributed to the compilation of this book and to my understanding of spelling within the context of the writing process.

Finally, my thanks are due to the staff in the library at Edge Hill College of Higher Education; they were most co-operative during my research of relevant literature.

The author and publishers would also like to thank the following for permission to reproduce material in this volume: Academic Press Ltd.; Allyn and Bacon for *The Beginnings of Writing* by C. Temple, R. Nathan, F. Temple and N. A. Burris; Blackwell Publishers; Cambridge University Press for *The Teaching of English from the Sixteenth Century to 1870* (1987) by I. Michael; Collins Educational for *Machines, Money and Men* by D. P. Titley; Harvard University Press for *Gnys at Wrk: a child learns to read and write* (1980) by G. Bissex; Heinemann for *Signposts to Spelling* by J. Pollock; HMSO for material reproduced with the permission of the Controller of Her Majesty's Stationery Office; Educational Review for *Spelling, Task and Learner*; International Reading Association for *Developmental and Cognitive Aspects of Learning to Spell* by E. H. Henderson and J. W. Beers; Lawrence Erlbaum Associates Ltd. for *Learning to Read: basic research and its implications* by L. Rieben and C. A. Perfetti and *Phonological Skills and Learning to Read* by U. Goswami and P. Bryant; LDA: Duke Street, Wisbech, Cambs. for *Joining the ABC* (ISBN 0 905114 72 8) by C. Cripps and R. Cox; Longman Group UK for *Breakthrough to Literacy* by D. Mackay, B. Thompson and P. Schaub; Manchester University Press for *A History of English Spelling* by D. G. Scragg; National Curriculum Council; Penguin Books Ltd. for *Five Hundred Years of Printing* by S. H. Steinberg, *Our Language* by S. Potter and *The English Language* by

D. Crystal; Stanley Thornes for *Handwriting: the way to teach it* by R. Sassoon.

1   *Perspectives on spelling*

The introduction of the National Curriculum (September 1989) has provided the basis and opportunity for a uniform description of the attainments and progess of pupils through all stages of schooling; it is a very positive step forward to find such specific references to spelling included in its Attainment Targets and Programmes of Study. The teaching of spelling has for some time, and much to the chagrin of some parents and employers, been a somewhat nebulous area of the English Curriculum, and very much dependent upon the importance placed upon it by individual schools. Indeed, as recently as 1984, a report from the DES listed its objectives in writing for pupils aged 7 years, yet no reference was made to spelling (DES, 1984, p. 6). The list was headed by the ability to write legibly; this was followed by a variety of writing tasks, and concluded by referring to pupils' ability to use full-stops and capital letters. Moreover, the same report, when considering writing objectives to be reached by 11 years, included a wider range of written activities in its list and a wider consideration of 'audience', yet the only reference to spelling was in the statement that pupils should:

> Exercise sufficient control over spellings, punctuation
> (at least the full-stop, question mark and comma) syntax
> and handwriting to communicate their meaning
> effectively. (p. 8)

Little wonder that methods of teaching spelling have, until recently, vacillated between rigorous (but not always relevant) learning of weekly word lists, and *ad hoc* consideration of certain spellings from time to time!

It is likely that this latter attitude to spelling may have resulted from the generally adverse reactions of teacher training colleges in the 1960s to the spelling lists and tests which were so popular in many schools from the 1930s up to (and beyond) the 1950s. For example, Fred Schonell's *The Essential Spelling List* (first published in 1932, and reprinted 29 times) was designed to equip teachers with a structured and graded system for teaching spelling to children of all ages and abilities. It was discarded by many schools in the 1960s because educational theory considered such

1

lists to be 'adult' or 'teacher' centred rather than 'child' centred; also, spellings drills and dictation exercises were considered to be not only time-consuming, but also non-productive, since the trend was to view the acquisition of correct spelling habits as something which occurred incidentally without being given overt attention, or to use Margaret Peters' expression, it was thought that spelling would be 'caught' rather than 'taught'. However, it is interesting to note that the Scottish Council for Research in Education (1961) did not follow the English trends and maintained that, with reference to the teaching of spelling, systematic methods achieved better and lasting results.

Of course, there are some children for whom our spelling system seems to cause few or no problems, and for whom spelling seems to be a skill which has been learned almost incidentally. We usually find, though, that such children have been encouraged by their parents to be aware of the everyday literacy around them from a very early age. There are also, however, children who have had little or no parental encouragement (in terms of literacy) and who may, unless given explicit instruction in spelling, experience difficulties with their spelling; others may have assumed that spelling is not important and may continue to disregard standard spelling not only as they progress through primary school, but also as they progress through secondary school. By then, their 'misspelling habits' have often become firmly established.

Indeed, my work with students of all ages in further and higher education reveals that an alarming proportion of them evidence deeply 'entrenched' misspellings in their written work, and it is much more difficult to erase such misspellings from their memories than to help them to learn new spellings related to their special subject areas.

Of course, in terms of comprehending written work which contains many spelling errors, we can generally understand or guess the message being communicated. There is, for example, little difficulty in comprehending the boy aged 14 years who wrote: 'My uncel viseted us and sed that I cold see his noow moter. It's a pawsh.' The point is that the pupil himself had become increasingly aware of his limitations in writing tasks and had lost confidence in himself as a writer. According to his father, he had once apparently enjoyed writing, especially as an infant and a lower junior, but since his school took the 'incidental' or 'caught' view of learning spelling, little attempt was made to correct his misspellings. Unfortunately, his parents were not able to provide much help since his father was a seaman and away for much of the time, and his mother was herself a poor speller. The older he grew, and particularly in the secondary school, the more he became ashamed (and was made to feel ashamed) of his written work; teachers told him to use a dictionary to check all his spellings. Yet, how does one look up 'said' if one thinks that it is spelled 'sed', or 'new' if one thinks that it is spelled 'noow'? Also, what about words which begin with silent letters, such as writing, knock, hour and honestly? Moreover, what if one has not been taught to use a dictionary effectively? In fact, the only reason that this pupil made the effort to write the preceding information was because, as he said, 'I wanted to have something to write that I could be proud of.' Needless to say, it was the 'pawsh' of which he was proud!

This example is reflected by an alarming proportion of young people who have been at some time given the idea that attention to spellings, punctuation and grammar need not be a major concern as 'all will fit into place' at some later date. Students who label themselves as 'poor spellers' are certainly very evident in classes in ABE (Mudd, 1990b). Indeed, a National Child Development Study (1983) revealed that one in ten of a sample of 12,534 23 year olds admitted to having problems with reading, writing and spelling. One such student (in her early 40s) wrote an account of her experiences and feelings prior to coming to evening class. Her work included the statement:

> Because my spelling and reading were below standard, I
> would not allow anyone to know that I was so bad through
> sheer embarrassment and fear that they would ridicule me.
> I must add that because I was so quiet the teachers did
> not try to push me or help me through the weak subjects in
> my schooling. They seemed to leave me at the back of the
> classroom to get on with my work.

This is just a brief extract from M's work; she undertook to write the text *only* because she knew she would receive personal individual help from a volunteer tutor. The work was thoroughly discussed, revised and corrected; it was commenced in October 1991 and completed in December 1991.

On the completion of her work, M said that she had got her resentment out of her system and was at last ready to make up for her 'lost' education. Since M was in her early 40s, it is worthy of note that her education occurred between the 1950s and 1960s (perhaps 'between' teaching philosophies in spelling). Though her English (in terms of spelling, punctuation and grammar) was at a considerably higher level than that of the boy aged 14 years, her self-image was certainly no higher than his. These two examples serve to underline what Margaret Peters (1987) has maintained since the 1960s, that the child who can spell is free to write with confidence, and that, conversely, the child who cannot spell often develops a poor self-image. There are, of course, children who are poor spellers who write at length and with apparent confidence but, as has been shown, as they grow older, their awareness of their shortcomings in the writing task generally inhibits any desires to write. On the other hand, good spellers often regard this attribute as a status symbol and usually view writing tasks as positive undertakings.

The two preceding examples also reinforce the findings of Peter Mortimore *et al.* (1988). His research was not concerned with spelling alone – it was concerned with probing the general effectiveness, or otherwise, of 50 junior schools. His findings highlight the importance of helping children to become successful learners and to regard themselves as successful learners while still in the junior school:

> We still believe the years between 7 and 11 to be particularly important since children are still able to change their view of themselves as good learners. We know from our other work on transition that, as children move into secondary schools, this flexibility diminishes. (p. 264)

Mortimore also found that structured teaching was more successful in motivating pupils and promoting effective learning than less structured teaching. He went on to say:

> In the structured sessions that we observed, teachers sought to provide a considerable degree of freedom for pupils, but did so within a well defined framework. (p. 268)

Thus, this book aims to illustrate how infant and junior teachers (from reception to year 6) may take a structured approach to the teaching of spelling while, at the same time, allowing for different levels of spelling development within a class. Such approaches should help childen to feel confident about their ability to communicate effectively in writing long before they leave their junior schools.

In their early school days in infant schools, spelling instruction is usually less structured or formal since young children generally spell according to the sound of words as *they* hear them ('toow' for 'two', 'becoz' for 'because' etc); this invented spelling of novice writers (which will be discussed in Chapters 3 and 4) is a vital part of their development in writing since it indicates to the teacher the writer's understanding of the writing process. However, changes in approaches to the teaching of spelling are exemplified by the National Curriculum (DES, 1990) which, while acknowledging the importance of novice writers' invented spellings, states: 'Teachers should help children to develop from invented spelling towards conventional accuracy' (English, B8, 3.1). The National Curriculum goes on to suggest that teachers of spelling should encourage 'the development of visual memory' (English, B8, 3.2), and that at a later stage they should make 'spellings and etymology the subject of investigative work' so that children may be helped to make 'connections between the language they use and that with which they are still experimenting' and 'Adolescents should be encouraged to recognise that proficient users of language continue to refer to dictionaries, thesauruses and spellcheckers' (English B8, 3.4).

These recommendations (and others like them) are, in my opinion, very positive and their implementation should help novice writers to become proficient users of written (and oral) language. They should, subsequently, reduce the numbers of adults of all ages who are so lacking in confidence and self-esteem that only the bravest attempt to improve their basic literacy skils in Adult Education Centres (and improvement becomes increasingly difficult with age, despite the one to one tuition in many centres). However, despite its suggestions for promoting accuracy in spelling, the National Curriculum is rather vague about exactly *how* teachers teach spelling and its related skills. For example:

- How do teachers help writers with the transition of invented to traditional spelling?

- How do teachers help children to look carefully at, and recall, the visual form of words?

- How to teachers help children to use dictionaries speedily and to locate the etymology of words?

- How do teachers help children with specific spelling difficulties?

In 1992, David Pascall wrote to John Patten (Secretary of State for Education) on behalf of the National Curriculum Council stating the case for revising the English order. He acknowledged the Council's support for the 'significant strengths' of English in the National Curriculum, but added that the knowledge and skills involved in speaking, listening, reading and writing needed to 'be defined more explicitly and rigorously'. The letter was concluded by various recommendations (ten in total) which included defining and placing more emphasis on: 'the basic skills of handwriting, spelling and grammar in the programmes of study and statements of attainment for Key Stages 1 and 2' (p. 12, item iv).

The Council also recommended that the current Attainment Targets 4 (spelling), 5 (handwriting) and 4/5 (presentation) should be: 'amalgamated into one attainment target, AT3, entitled "Writing including spelling, grammar and handwriting".' This will ensure that the importance of these basic skills is clear to pupils, teachers and parents while emphasising the close relationship between the mechanics of writing and the use of writing to communicate meaning. It seems clear then that teachers need more explicit guidance in the effective teaching of spelling – spelling which is considered, along with handwriting, as an integral part of the writing process. Such teaching will be discussed in Chapter 6, and in Chapters 7, 8 and 9, which put forward ideas for the effective teaching of spelling with respect to infants, juniors and children with spelling difficulties. We should not forget that what we teach, or rather think we are teaching, is not necessarily understood, learned or assimilated by the learner (Mudd, 1987 and 1990) and so emphasis will be on making instruction explicit. Chapter 5 considers the assessment of spelling (progress and difficulties) within the writing process, for as Mortimore *et al.* (1988, p. 268) observed, teachers should: 'include some time for an audit of which tasks have been achieved and of what has been learned.'

Chapter 4 looks briefly at the development of children's writing as a whole, beginning with their early 'invented' spellings. The aim of Chapter 3 is to give teachers and students an idea of some past and present methods of teaching spelling and writing.

However, before considering how we may teach spelling effectively and deal with potential difficulties in our standard spelling system, perhaps we should consider briefly the origins and development of our language so that anyone interested in the teaching (or learning) of traditional spelling may understand more about the many and varied influences which have interacted to produce our unique language, and what are often termed as the inconsistencies in our writing/spelling system, that is, our orthography.

Thus, Chapter 2 will outline how other languages, especially French, Latin and Greek have, during the past 2,000 years, gradually influenced our current language and spellings. The chapter will also refer to American spellings and to the increasing use of acronyms and vocabulary related to technology in our language.

2 The development of the English language

Our language has its origins in the Indo-European language (sometimes called Indo-Germanic, or Aryan) which was spoken some 5,000 years ago by nomads living in the plains of what is now the Ukraine and Southern Russia, and so is related to most of the other languages of Europe and Western Asia. Though it was not a written language, we can hear relationships in the sound of some words, for example, brother (German *Bruder* and Latin *Frater*) and mother (German *Mutter* and Latin *Mater*).

The Celts

The land we now know as Britain was then inhabited by Celts (who were also to be found in Gaul and Spain). Many of the Cornish Celts later found new homes in Brittany where Breton is still a living language, whereas Cornish died out in the eighteenth century. Manx was used in the isolated village of Cregneish, about 2 miles from Port Erin until 1960 when its last speakers died and their cottages were turned into a museum. Scottish Gaelic is still spoken in the Highlands and Western Isles but by less than 100,000 people. Welsh and Irish are living languages though most Celtic speaking Welsh and Irish are bilingual.

Some Celtic words are still widely used, for example: crag (related to Old Welsh, *creik*, a rock); glen (related to Old Irish, *glend*); slogan (from Scottish Gaelic, *sluagh-ghairm*, a war-cry); whisky (Scottish Gaelic from *uisge beatha*, literally, water of life). Gaelic refers to any of the closely related languages of the Celts in Ireland, Scotland or (formerly) the Isle of Man. As we shall see, however, the English language of today owes very little to the language of the Celts (or Ancient Britons).

Influences of Rome, Latin and Christianity

With the arrival of the Romans in the south of England in 55 BC under the leadership of Julius Caesar, many Celts withdrew westwards and northwards into Cornwall, Ireland and Scotland; the remaining Celts were thus mainly in the south east and became known as Britons, that is, of Celtic origin. After a brief return to Rome because of invaders in their own country, the Romans came again to our shores in AD 43 and intermarried with the Britons. During the 400 or so years when Britain was a province of the Roman Empire, Latin is presumed to have been spoken in the cities and larger country villas (Latin was the name of the language used in Ancient Rome and the Roman Empire). Many Latin inscriptions have been discovered which were probably composed by army officers and more ambitious artisans who scratched graffiti on tiles and earthenware. However, such inscriptions do not necessarily testify to a widespread use of Latin (Potter, 1982, p. 18).

The coming of St Augustine in AD 597 heralded the subsequent conversion of our island to Latin Christianity. It is interesting to note, though, that Old English (OE), which may be said to stem from about AD 450, was comparatively free from words of foreign origin. Naturally, it had incorporated a certain number of Latin words, chiefly relating to the institutions and rituals of the church, for example: bishop (from OE *biscop*, from late Latin *espiscopus*); candle (OE *candel*, from Latin *candela*); creed (from OE *creda*, from Latin *credo*, I believe); mass (from OE *mæsse*, from Church Latin *missa*). Generally speaking, writers in this period preferred to invent new equivalent forms from native words, even for the technical terms of Christian theology. Thus, it is of interest to note the estimated dates (*Collins English Dictionary*, 1991) of the introduction of the following examples of Latinate words into our language (C = century): communion (C14 – *communis*, common); crucifix (C13 – *crux*, a cross); sacrament (C12 – *sacramentum*, a vow). Words related to the Roman civilisation include: aqueduct (C16 – *aqua*, water, plus *ducere*, to convey); castle (C11 – *castrum*, a fort); village (C15 – *villa*). The Latin word *castra*, became *ceaster*, the OE word for a Roman fortified town, and it survives in the endings of many place-names, such as Chester, Lancaster, Leicester and Winchester. It may be said that the influence of Latin into our language was more evident after the coming of the Normans in 1066 than by the earlier Roman occupation. As we shall see later, the French-speaking Normans were greatly influenced by the Latin culture.

The Romans remained here for over 400 years. In the fifth century, the Roman legions were recalled to defend their homeland which was under attack from East European invaders. Therefore, Britain, a fertile land with few inhabitants, was left to fend for itself.

Anglo-Saxon influences

During the fifth and sixth centuries, Germanic tribes, who had heard that the land here was good for farming and that the Roman legions had departed, invaded Britain and many settled here. These tribes included Angles (from Schleswig), Saxons (from Holstein), and Jutes (from Jutland), and they spoke substantially the same language. When they first arrived (about AD 449) Britain was basically a Celtic-speaking land. A whole generation had passed away since the Romans had left in AD 410 and there is little evidence regarding how many people spoke and understood Latin. The invaders established themselves in different parts of the country, and in consequence of local separation their original (albeit fairly minimal) divergences of speech gradually became wider, so that in three or four centuries the kinds of English spoken in varying areas became markedly different. There were four main dialects (not languages) spoken in the areas of Wessex (south west England) and Kent, both occupied mainly by Saxons and Jutes, Mercia (an area that eventually comprised most of the Midlands, occupied by Angles and Saxons), and Northumberland (occupied by Angles). In the main, though, all the people who had become termed English (and speaking what we now call Old English) differed little in their vocabulary despite the considerable diversity of pronunciation. Likewise, spelling systems, though differing slightly, were not too dissimilar. Among the many Saxon words (OS = Old Saxon) which have remained with us are: wold – rolling, upland country (from OE *weuld*, related to OS *wald*); bridge (from OE *Brycg*, from OS *bruggia*); back (from OE *boec*, from OS *baec*); mother (from OE *modor*, from OS *modar*).

St Augustine (the Roman Benedictine missionary who became the first Archbishop of Canterbury) was responsible for the resumption of contact with the life and thought of the Mediterranean. The written word was important in spreading the word of Christianity, and so it may be said that the coming of Christianity was responsible for beginnings of English orthography (conventional spelling). England became a home of learning and especially England north of the Humber. Hild, Abbess of Whitby, was the best educated of all Anglo-Saxon women; similarly, Bede (surnamed the Venerable) was an English monk and ecclesiastical historian, born at Wearmouth in the seventh century, and he wrote the 'Ecclesiastical history of England' in Latin. This was later translated into English by Alfred the Great (King of Wessex from AD 871–99). From about the seventh century, Old English began to be written using the Latin alphabet (it was probably introduced by Irish missionaries). The

Latin alphabet was, however, inadequate to express some of the more complex phonological (sound) systems of the Old English dialects, and so new symbols were added, such as æ ('a' joined to 'e'), and also digraphs (two letters combined to form a single sound) were introduced for consonant sounds that were unknown to the Romans, for example, /*th*/. Although there is considerable agreement about the orthography as applied to the Old English sound system, there is considerable variation in spelling forms between one dialect and another, and between scribes. Nevertheless, as Scragg (1975, p. 14) suggests, it is possibly the early stabilisation of our spelling system which is at the root of our present orthographic arguments. He goes on to state:

> Though, in later centuries English spelling was considerably influenced by conventions of later systems, particularly those of French, the native tradition was never entirely lost, and our spelling is thus the result of the overlaying for nearly a thousand years of one tradition upon another.

Viking influences

'Viking' was a name given to the Scandinavian (including Danes) sea-rovers and pirates who, from the eighth to the tenth centuries, plundered the shores chiefly of western Europe. They founded Normandy in north-western France, and colonised much of the British Isles, Iceland, Greenland and Russia. The coming of the Vikings (men of the *viks* or creeks) to Lindisfarne and its subsequent sacking put an end to monastic learning in the north. King Alfred saved Wessex from a similar fate by inviting scholars from Mercia and Wales and abroad to help him to revive learning in the south. Interestingly, it is only from the time of King Alfred that records have been found which are sufficiently full to follow the history of our spelling in any detail. He also made a treaty with the Danish Vikings after fighting many battles with them with varying degrees of success. The treaty permitted them to settle in the northern, central and eastern parts of Anglo-Saxon England. These areas became known as 'Danelaw' since Danish law and customs were observed there.

In 991, Ethelred the Unready (956–1016), King of England from 978, imposed a tax on land to try to pay off the Danes from the shores of England. It was a tax of one shilling (later two) on every hide of land (a hide is a variable unit or area of land, considered to be adequate to support a household), and was called 'Danegeld' – perhaps the very first form of income tax! Interestingly, 'unready' does not (as thought by some) mean one who is not ready; it means one who does not rule well or listen to advice (OE *rædan*, to rule, advise or explain). 'Geld', meaning a tax (OE *gield*, is related to Old High German *gelt* meaning income or retribution). As might have been expected, the Danes took the money and returned for more. Eventually, the famous King Cnut (Canute) who ruled Norway and Denmark, became King of all England from 1016–35; he reputedly ruled wisely and well.

Among the many Viking words which are still used today, we find: beck, a stream (from OE *becc*, from Old Norse (ON) *bekkr*); hit (from OE *hittan*, from ON *hitta*); knock (from OE *cnoocian*, from ON *knooka*; note that the initial 'c' and 'k' were pronounced originally); slaughter (from OE *sleaht*, from ON *slattar*, to hammer); toft, a homestead (from ON *topt*; as in Lowestoft).

Before A D 1000 we were known as Angelcym (Angle race), and after A D 1000 our land became known as Engaland (land of Angles); our language was Englisc ('sc' was then pronounced more or less as 'sh').

Old English may be said to stem originally (and approximately) from A D 449 onwards with the arrival of the Angles, Saxons, Jutes and, later, the Vikings; it lasted until after the arrival of the Normans in 1066. Our Celtic language was greatly influenced by these peoples from the north, In fact, a documentary series shown on television (BBC 2, 1986) stated that our most familiar words are generally derived from Old English. I have amended and abbreviated a text which the documentary film used to illustrate this point; the text showed how the diary of a common man living in Mercia before 1100 might have read:

> I have lived and worked all of my life deep in the heart of Mercia. I must walk very slowly so as not to frighten the game. The buck falls to the ground. There will be a great deal of meat for my wife and children today.

(However, later in this chapter, I will be referring to the fact that Henry Bradley (1987) maintains that words of Old English origin are outnumbered in novels, papers, magazines, etc., by words derived from foreign languages). The words in the text above have been transcribed into Modern English. Old English prose (and certainly poetry) had the aspect of a foreign language and Bradley (1987, p. 7) illustrates this point with an example taken from a sermon by Ælfric (Abbot of Cerne) who died about 1025.

Thā the ne gelȳfath thurh āgenne cyre hī scoriath, nā thurh gewyrd; for-than-the gewyrd nis nān thing būton lēas wēna	They who do not believe refuse through their own choice, not through fate, because fate is nothing but a false notion.

As Bradley says, it is impossible to give any complete rules for Old English pronunciation; however, included in his suggestions for giving the reader an approximate notion of the sounds of the language are:

g to be sounded like *y* in 'young', though the g in āg should be sounded like g in 'good'

f to be sounded like *v*

c to be sounded like *k*

sc to be sounded like *sh*

the final e in āgenne to be sounded like the e in taker (it is not 'silent')

ā to be pronounced like the a in 'father'; an unmarked a has a shorter sound

Bradley goes on to make observations on some of the words in the text (p. 8) stating that *Thā* corresponds to our 'that', while *the* stands for 'who', 'whom' or 'which'. In *ge-lȳf-ath*, the middle syllable is the same as the second syllable in 'believe'; the verb *ge-lȳf-an* corresponds to the German *g-laub-en*. *Ne* stands for 'not' and is put before the verb in Old English. It is interesting also to compare *thurh*, 'through', with the German *durch* as well as to compare *Āgenne*, 'own', with the German *eigen*. *Ge-wyrd*, 'fate', is the word which in later English became 'weird'. *Nān thing* is 'none thing'; in Old English, two negatives did not make an affirmative, but were combined for emphasis as in Greek.

As has been stated, our language was influenced greatly by northern invaders, and the influences of the German language is seen clearly in the short extract from the Abbot of Cerne's sermon at the top of this page.

Norman influences

Edward the Confessor, who was King of England after Canute from 1042–66, had grown up in Normandy. A rather feeble monarch, he showed favours to the Normans and also promised succession to the English throne to William of Normandy, despite having earlier recognised Harold, son of Earl Godwin of Wessex, as the heir. (It is probable that his change of allegiance to William occurred during the exile of Godwin and his family.)

After the famous Norman Conquest at Hastings in 1066, William became King of England. In fact, *Nor-man-d-y* (or Northmen's land) was another Danelaw established in France; the Normans were mostly descendants of Norsemen who had shed their Scandinavian speech and became converts to Latin culture and to the French language. William I tried to learn English, but his age (he was 43 years old) and his busy life prevented any significant progress and, in the main, he retained his French language. Moreover, for the next three centuries, all the kings of England spoke French and, with the exception of Henry I (1068–1135) who married Eadfyth (this name being later changed to Matilda), no king of England until Edward IV (1461–83) who married Elizabeth Woodville, had married a wife from our island. It was Henry I (1399–1413) who became the first king after the Norman Conquest to have English as his mother tongue.

French and Latin were used in church services and words such as bible, communion, crucifix and sacrament (all from Church Latin) were in general use. By approximately 1180, there was intermarriage between the English and the Normans, and so an Anglo/Norman knight might have an English wife, though his wife, children and serfs were likely to speak only English. It was not until the 1200s that the French language began to be learned and read widely, especially among the upper and/or educated classes. As Bradley (1987, p. 57) says:

> The knowledge of French gave access to the rich literature of the continent; from the thirteenth to the fifteenth century a large portion of the literature of England consisted of translations of French romance and the native poetry was powerfully influenced by the French models.

The French used in England subsequent to the Norman Conquest was influenced by the dialect of Normandy and Picardy, while the accession of the Angevin dynasty under Henry II in 1154 introduced the dialect of central France into England; and the latter soon became the language of the court and fashionable society. Simeon Potter (1982, p. 35) quotes the chronicler, Robert of Gloucester, who wrote, 'Vor bote a man conne fress me telp of him lute' ('unless a man knows French, one counts of him little').

Certainly, the French language had a great impact on our vocabulary, and words for power and authority were (and are) mainly French in origin. For example: royal (C14 Old French (OF) *roial* from Latin (L) *regalis*); sovereign (C13 from OF *soverain*, from Vulgar Latin *superanus*); govern (C14, from OF *gouverner*, from L *gubernare*, to steer). The English word gaol is interesting in that it is from the Old Norman French word *gaole* and also from Old French *jaiole* (in the United States, the spelling is jail).

The French language is also in great evidence among our culinary terms; in fact, in Scott's *Ivanhoe* the Saxon serfs, Wamba and Gurth, discuss the fact that the live ox, swine and calf are referred to in English, whereas those of the cooked meats are in French, that is, beef, pork and veal (*boeuf, porc, veel*). And, of course, in the 'best' English restaurants (a word used from the nineteenth century; its origin is in the French word, *restaurer*, to restore) menus are generally written in French (*menu* is also a French word meaning a detailed list). Similarly, many of our culinary terms testify to the influence of French cuisine, for example, boil (C13 from OF *boillir*); fry (C13 from OF *frire*); roast (C13 from OF *rostir*); toast (C14 from OF *toster*). Also, we still often see RSVP (*Repondez s'il vous plaît*) on invitations and Messrs (*Messieurs*) in everyday correspondence.

From about 1100 until approximately 1450, the French language greatly influenced our own Old English language, and we refer to the English of this period as Middle English. Also, comparatively little written English survives from 1100 to 1300. One effect of bilingualism in England was that a large proportion of present-day English vocabulary is derived from the French. According to Scragg (1975), about 40 per cent of our dictionary words are French in derivation, though an average English sentence contains a smaller percentage since most of our basic and commonest words are English. Scragg also states (p. 51) that Anglo-Norman practice provided a major influence on English spelling. However, the second half of the fourteenth century also saw the emergence of factors which promoted the development and use of our own language; the first of these factors being the language used in Parliament, this being a term used first in the thirteenth century, originating from the Anglo-Latin, *parliamentum*, from OF *parlement*, from *parler* to speak. Simon de

Montfort, the son of a French count, came to England in 1230 where he inherited the earldom of Leicester from his grandmother; it was he who greatly influenced the development of Parliament.

The language of Parliament

October 1362 may be taken as a turning point in the development of English (Potter, 1982) since it was in that month that Parliament was first opened in English, and when all court proceedings were conducted in English (though enrolled or recorded in Latin). Law French, however, persisted much longer, and it was not abolished until 1731 by Act of Parliament. In fact, the French language still exists in, for example, the Royal Arms (*Dieu et mon droit*) and in the crest of the Garter (*Honi soi qui mal y pense*).

The language of Geoffrey Chaucer

Influential too in the development of the English language was Geoffrey Chaucer (about 1300–1400), our first great literary writer and best known for his unfinished cycle of *Canterbury Tales*, written about 1387. (Interestingly, the term 'canter' became widely used in the eighteenth century; it was short for 'Canterbury trot', the supposed pace at which pilgrims rode to Canterbury.) Like many other educated people of his time, Chaucer was trilingual (English, French and Latin) and he could, therefore, have written his works in any of these languages; however, he chose to write in English and so promoted our mother tongue.

William Caxton

Caxton (1420/4–91) was a translator, publisher and printer; he spent 30 years in Bruges, which was the central market of northern European commerce. In his leisure time he translated into English, books written in French, for example, *Recueil des histoires de Troy*. In order to publish books according to his taste, he decided to learn the craft of printing for himself. This he did with another printer in Cologne (1471–2) and in 1473 he was able to set up his own printing press there. In 1476 he returned to England to set up a further press near Westminster. *Aesop's Fables* were translated by Caxton and printed by him in 1483. Like Chaucer, Caxton's main importance lies in the fact that among over 90 books printed by him, 74 were in English. In addition, Caxton is important in the development of our language because it was he who helped to standardise it through the medium of printing. He overcame the perplexing and potential confusion of the varied Middle English dialects by 'adopting' the speech of the Home Counties and London.

Prior to the invention of printing, spelling had been mainly phonetic (spelling according to sound), and so spellings had differed widely according to local dialects. (Monasteries, however, had always striven for some uniformity.) It may be said that the mass circulation of the printed work in England thus spread the use of the vernacular. Spelling reformers argue that our spelling system does not often accurately represent the visual aspect of letters in words, and it may be said to be illogical. However, Steinberg (1961) states:

> The fundamental fallacy of all spelling reformers is that the function of the printed or written word is to represent the spoken word. The true function surely of the printed or written word is to convey meaning, and to convey the same meaning to as many people as possible. (p. 126)

Among interesting (and relevant) spelling developments in the fifteenth century was the introduction of the *gh* blend, which has survived in a great many words in which the former 'c' and 'x' sounds were once heard (as in the German words *ich*, *licht* and *ach* or the Scottish word *loch*). Examples of such words include: high, ought, night, bough; in some northern dialects the *gh* sound is still retained. Indeed, Scots remains the one British dialect which may be represented today by a consistent, traditional orthography (Scragg, 1975, p. 37). Scragg also points out that it was in the early *thirteenth* century that manuscripts were found illustrating the doubling of consonants to show that a preceding vowel in a closed syllable was short, for example: *wille* (wishes); *witt* (wit); *sette* (laid down). In contemporary spelling books, 'doubling' is used before adding suffixes to words containing one syllable in which the consonant follows a single short vowel, for example: tap/ped; hid/den; rub/ber. Doubling also occurs in some words of two syllables (depending upon where the stress occurs), for example: admit/ted; begin/ner; occur/ring.

In the fourteenth century, long vowels became associated with a final mute *e*, for example mete, mate, mute; but some words which had doubled their vowel to indicate a long vowel sound, were still retained, for example: book, spoon, seek. Since these words are still spelled the same way today, they add to the inconsistency of our spelling system.

It was in the thirteenth century that the late Latin practice of using *o* for *u* caused some interchange of the two graphemes in French and later in English. Thus, *o* replaced *u* in a large number of words with a short vowel; for example: come, some, Somerset, monk, son, tongue, wonder, honey, worry, above, dove, love (Scragg, 1975, p. 43).

The language of the Bible

By the fifteenth century, written English was becoming recognisable as the English we use today, and among the works that have further contributed to the formation of Modern English, an important place should be given to the translations of the Bible, from those of William Tyndale and Miles Coverdale, in the early sixteenth century, to the King James version of 1611. It could be said that William Tyndale (c.1494–1536) did more than anyone else to create a simple, all-purpose prose style. Potter (1982) writes

> . . . his gifts as a writer of simple musical narrative were fully revealed in his translation of the New Testament in 1525. Like all masters of language he wrote for the ear and not the eye. (p. 53)

In fact, one-third of the King James Bible is said to be worded exactly as Tyndale's language. For example, a word used by Tyndale (and now quite indispensable in our language) is 'beautiful'. Although he did not 'invent' the word (it originated from OF *biau*, beautiful), it was its introduction by Tyndale into the Bible that brought the word into general use. Tyndale was also the first to use the combination of words in, for example, 'peacemaker', and to use 'elder' in its ecclesiastical sense (in the English Bible, 'priest' never occurs as the designation of a Christian minister).

The fact that the Bible was, for centuries, the most widely read and most frequently quoted of books made it a fruitful source of changes of meaning; also its indirect effect on the English vocabulary has been progressive down to recent times. Many words which, in the natural course of things, would have become obsolete, have been preserved because of their occurrence in familiar passages of scripture. Examples include: apparel/raiment (dress/clothes); quick (living); damsel (young woman).

Similarly, many phrases from the Bible (mostly literal renderings of Hebrew and Greek) have assumed the character of English idioms and thus we may say, 'to cast pearls before swine' or 'the eleventh hour' without realising the nature of their origins (Potter, 1982).

The revival of learning

After the beginning of the sixteenth century, the revival of Greek learning in western Europe opened up a new source from which the English vocabulary could be enriched. It should be noted though that long before this time most European languages contained Greek words, such as geography (from *ge*, earth); theology (from *theos*, god); logic (from *logikos*, concerning speech or reasoning), which had come through the medium of Latin. In the sixteenth and seventeenth centuries Latin was, however, still the common vehicle of the literature of science and philosophy, and so new technical terms of Greek etymology were often treated as though they had passed through a Latin channel. For example, Greek adjectives were usually Anglicised, like Latin adjectives, by the addition of the suffix -ous, -an, or -al, and so we wrote: autonomous (not autonomos), and diaphanous (not diaphanes).

Greek technical vocabulary has always been noted for its lucidity and precision, and thus it is not surprising that when a word is wanted to denote some concept peculiar to modern science, the most convenient way of obtaining it is usually to coin a new Greek compound or derivative. Fairly recently coined words of Greek etymology include names of diseases and processes or instruments of modern invention. For example, we have: leukaemia (*leukos*, white; *haima*, blood); telegraph (*tele*, far; *graphein*, to write); telephone (*phone*, voice or sound); stethoscope (*stethos*, breast; *skopein*, to look at). Such words are used internationally since the custom of forming compounds from Greek elements is common in all civilised countries of Europe and Africa.

The classical Renaissance of the sixteenth century also led to a wholesale importation of Latin words, and many French-derived words became re-shaped on Latin models; thus Chaucerian words like *parfit* and *verdit* became perfect (L *perfectus*) and verdict (L *verdictum*). Also *dette* became debt (L *debitum*), *doute* became doubt (L *dubitare*), and *vittles* (from OF *vitaille*) became victuals (from L *victualia*, provisions). Similarly, *iland* (ME from OE *ieg*) became wrongly associated with the Latin word *insula*, and so was written as island. It is both interesting and very relevant (especially with respect to the teaching of spelling) to note that though many spellings were thus changed, their pronunciations remained the same (hence the misspellings of those who spell mainly according to sound). Moreover, during the Renaissance period, Latin and English became increasingly *blended*, and suffixes such as -ment (L *mentum*) were added to our Middle English words, for example: acknowledgement, amazement, merriment. Native compounds with the Latin suffix -ation (L *atus* and *ion*) first appeared in the eighteenth century, for example: flirtation, invitation, sensation, starvation.

Clearly, the influence of Greek and Latin had profound effects upon our language and led to an accession of new words, often of a learned and polysyllabic kind, which, when used to excess by less critical writers, who wished mainly to impress rather than inform, earned their authors the label users of 'inkhorn terms'. An inkhorn term is an affectedly learned and obscure borrowing from another language, especially Greek or Latin (*Collins English Dictionary*, 1991). Potter (1982, p. 48) refers to Thomas Wilson, whose *Art of Rhetorique* (1553) reprimands those who 'affect straunge ynke-horne termes' and who 'seeke so far for outlandish English that they forget altogether their mothers language'.

Consistency in spelling

Although it has been stated that Caxton helped in the development of our language, he, like other early printers, did little to encourage conformity of spelling since they did not have linguistic backgrounds. In fact, Scragg (1975, p. 66) shows how Caxton's translation of *The Historie of Jason* published in 1477, contains in one very brief sample the same words spelled in different ways, for example: hye, hyghe; hadde, had; sayd, sayde. However, during the sixteenth century, the products of the best printers began to reflect the spellings of professional scribes of that period. Thus, between 1550 and 1650, there was tremendous growth of universal acceptance by *printers* of the stable spelling system, that with very few modifications is in use today (Scragg, 1975, p. 67). Interestingly though, there was a lack of consistency in private writing during the reign of Elizabeth I (1558–1603), and so we hear of Queen Elizabeth and Shakespeare being labelled as 'poor spellers' because their spellings varied considerably, yet there was no official spelling standardisation which could have helped them to become 'good spellers'.

Despite the work of scholars like Mulcaster and Coote in the sixteenth century, it was not until the seventeenth century that spellings became consistent. An important publication of the eighteenth century was the *Dictionary of English Language* (1755) by Samuel Johnson, and in the nineteenth century 'literary' homes always included the book (as well as the Bible and Shakespeare's works) in their libraries. Contrary to the opinion of some, Johnson was not responsible for the anomalies of English spelling. As we have seen, he simply recorded established convention.

Influences from other languages

Contacts with foreign peoples from the 1600s to the present day has resulted in a greatly increased English vocabulary. Indeed, our Modern English bears historical witness to the many words the English language has adopted from other tongues (Bradley, 1987). For example, the presence in our dictionaries of terms such as aria, fantasia, finale, intermezzo, oboe, opera, piano, fresco, graffito, replica, studio, should inform us that the Italians have been our teachers in music and fine arts. Similarly, terms such as avast, boom, buoy, cruiser, deck, hull, skipper, sloop, smack, are among the many words which give evidence to the fact that the Dutch people were once supreme in nautical matters.

From the Russian language we have adopted terms such as samovar, soviet, sputnik, steppe, vodka and, more recently, glasnost (openness), and perestroika (reconstruction). Everyday words adapted from Turkish include: kiosk, kaftan (or caftan) and horde. From China, we have the word tea and the names of various kinds of tea. More recently there has been an influx of words and phrases from the USA, Australia and New Zealand into our language (mainly as a result of the screening of their programmes on television and ease of travel to those countries). Thus, our language includes words and expressions such as bread, crook (as in 'I feel crook'), fink, gas, zilch, heavy man, stay cool man. And, of course, children and teenagers in particular are able (and usually very willing) to supply many more.

American spellings

The distinctive features of American orthography, which in some instances have been simplified, are mainly the result of the work of Noah Webster (1758–1843) whose *American Spelling Book* first appeared in 1783. As a teacher in the outskirts of New York, he was profoundly aware of the inconsistencies in English spelling, and was, at first, all set to make drastic changes in his dictionary (for example, *hed, proov, det, giv*). However, being a practical businessman and wanting to make money from his publication, Webster sought a market for his book on both sides of the Atlantic. Therefore, he agreed when his publisher suggested that he modify his changes. So we find, for example, -or instead of -our (favor, color); -er instead of -re (center, theater); -l instead of -ll (traveler, jewelry); -s instead of -c in nouns (defense, offense); and simplifications for words such as catalogue (catalog), cheque (check), programme (program). Webster's *New International Dictionary* is the official spelling guide of the Government Printing Office and the accepted authority in American courts.

Influences of advanced technology

With the development of computer and microchip technology, we find that our everyday language includes words such as computer, compact disc, fax (facsimile transmission), floppy disk, photocopier, plastic money, robotics, telex, word-processor, including the notorious scud missiles which were used in the Iran–Iraq war and the Gulf war.

Acronyms

For more than 20 years we have seen a tremendous increase in the number of acronyms (a pronounceable name made up of a series of the initial letters of words). We have, for example, ASH (Action on Smoking and Health); ERNIE (Electronic Random Number Indicator Equipment); DINKIE (Double Income No Kids), YUPPIES (Young Upwardly Mobile Professional – the 'ie' is added to the stem of the last two acronyms); and DUMP (Disposal of Unwanted Medicine and Pills). Frequently, people who use acronyms tend to forget (or indeed be unaware of) the actual words which are represented by the acronym; it is likely that few people realise that the word LASER is composed of the words: Light Amplification by Stimulated Emission of Radiation, or that the RADAR is composed of the words RAdio Detection And Ranging.

Summary

This chapter has traced very briefly the major influences and developments which have resulted in the English language of today. The increase of the English vocabulary by additions from so many sources has meant that words of native etymology are small in proportion compared to the total number of words given in our modern dictionaries. While acknowledging that not a quarter of the words in dictionaries are really familiar to the mass of well-educated readers, Bradley (1987) maintains:

> . . . even if we take the actual vocabulary of modern novels or newspaper articles, it still remains true that the words of Old English origin are far outnumbered by those derived from other tongues. (p. 70)

A very positive effect of the etymological diversity of our vocabulary has been to provide a language which is rich in words and expressions which may be used as alternatives to each other. As a general rule, we may say that when two words express the same idea, one of them being of native and the other of French or Latin etymology, the native word is the one that has the fuller emphasis and the greater richness of emotional suggestion (and/or sincerity), since native words tend to be those used by working people in their everyday lives. This knowledge is used by advertisers (and poets) who are seeking to sway the heart rather than convince the head. Note the effect (and warmth) of: home, love, good, friend, happiness, compared with: domicile, affection, commendable, acquaintance, felicity. However, it is not suggested that we give preference to words of Anglo-Saxon English in our speech or writing; the effective speaker or writer selects their vocabulary according to their purpose and audience. As Bradley (1987, p. 74) says of our language:

> . . . in skilled hands it is capable of a degree of precision and energy which can be equalled in few languages either ancient or modern.

In the Preface to *Collins English Dictionary* (1991, p. XXIII), David Brazil shows too the importance of the English language over a vast proportion of the world's people:

> Over the last five hundred years, the English language, formerly the language of a mere five or six million people living within the confines of the British Isles, has expanded to become the everyday speech of over three hundred million. Among the results of this expansion is the present status of English as the mother tongue of most of the

inhabitants of the vast ethnically diverse society of the United
States of America, and as the most important second
language of some fifty million in Southern Asia and a number
of the nations of Africa.

3 Spelling and writing: past and present approaches and views

Education in the 1800s

Towards the end of the nineteenth century, elementary schools were provided exclusively for children of the poor with the introduction of the 1870 Education Act. Even so, education did not become compulsory until 1876 and it was not free until 1899. Up to this time, education had to be bought by those who could afford it. The nature of teaching during this period left much to be desired when viewed from a modern perspective. Ian Michael (1987, pp. 226–7) states:

> Teachers' methods were determined principally by their views about children and about language. Children were thought to be unformed, empty . . . [and should be] receptive, but passive.

We shall see that the teaching methods described in the 1800s exemplify Michael's observations.

At the beginning of the nineteenth century, education was not compulsory and although most upper- and middle-class children received some teaching, the majority of working-class children were either illiterate or could barely read or write. There were old-established grammar schools and numerous small private schools for the middle classes who could not afford to send their children to public schools. While a few of the private schools offered a good education, others seem to have been horrific places, and most may recall Charles Dickens' caricature of such a school in *Nicholas Nickleby*; Nicholas observes Wackford Squeers, the headmaster of Dotheboys Hall, giving a demonstration of the practical teaching of spelling:

> C-l-e-a-n, clean, verb active, to make bright. W-i-n-d-e-r, winder, a casement. When a boy knows this out of a book, he goes and does it. (1953, p. 105, first pub. 1839)

With respect to working-class education, some charity schools had survived from the eighteenth century and also there were the Sunday Schools founded by Robert Raikes in 1780. These had spread rapidly in some large towns for, in addition to divinity, instruction was given in the 'three Rs'. Common, too, were the Dame schools where young children were looked after by old women for a fee of about 1½ old pence per week; despite the often cramped and dismal interiors of such 'schools', many of these women did manage to teach children to read and write. Teaching methods were usually based upon a cane or sweet philosophy, with application of either as appropriate!

In the early years of the nineteenth century, schools for the poor were begun by two religious societies: the British and Foreign Schools Society founded by Joseph Lancaster for Nonconformists, and the National Society founded by Andrew Bell for members of the Church of England. Both societies used the Bible as a textbook and much of the 'education' consisted of rote learning (knowledge acquired by repetition). Titley (1977, p. 146) refers to a school in Manchester with one thousand children and only three teachers. The teachers taught the school monitors sets of questions and responses; in turn the monitors passed on the questions and responses to the pupils. For example:

Monitor: You read the sentence 'the enamel is disposed in crescent-shaped ridges'. What is the enamel?
Boy: The hard shining part of the tooth.
Monitor: What do you mean by disposed?
Boy: Placed.
Monitor: The root of the word?
Boy: Pono, I place.
Monitor: What is crescent-shaped?
Boy: Shaped like a moon, before it is a half moon.

These 'unthinking' responses may (it is hoped!) be contrasted with the National Curriculum's recommendations to teachers to make spelling and etymology the subject of investigative work – work which is relevant to ongoing class topics. It is also hoped that teachers who undertake such investigative work are more informed about locating etymological sources than the teachers responsible for passing on information to monitors in the extract; the root of the word 'disposed' is attributed to the Latin word *pono*; in fact 'posed' (and 'disposed') has its origins in the fourteenth century and was derived from OF *poser* (to set in place), though it was *influenced* by the Latin word *ponere*, to place (*Collins English Dictionary*, 1991).

However, these schools did enable many children from working-class families to become literate. Even so, there were still large numbers of children who never went to school, and according to Titley (1977), in 1830 over 30 per cent of men and 40 per cent of women still signed the marriage register with a cross.

In 1860, Robert Lowe, the Minister for Education, introduced 'Payment by Results' by which the amount of money a school received from the government depended upon the numbers of children on the register and how well they did in an annual examination in reading, writing and arithmetic.

Of course, this usually meant that nothing was taught except the facts required and facts were often learned 'parrot' fashion, though it was claimed that most children did, at least, have a fairly sound knowledge of the 'three Rs'. (The key word in the last sentence is 'claimed' since there were no standardised tests and generally no records were kept of children who went to school, but who *failed* to learn to read and write.)

Similarly, children from middle-class families experienced learning by rote, and during the Victorian era (1831–1901) the Bible and John Bunyan's *Pilgrims Progress* held pride of place in most homes. Writing generally was restricted to copying extracts from the Bible or writing out poems and proverbs of an 'uplifting' or moral nature. Young girls often improved their knowledge of the alphabet, numbers, language, spelling and punctuation via the samplers which were worked for hours on end. (A sampler is a piece of embroidery worked in various stitches as evidence of proficiency. Often they were displayed on walls etc. See figure 3.1). Another child's typical sampler (seen in Rufford Old Hall, Lancashire) shows numbers from 0–10, the alphabet from A–Z, and a verse from a poem:

> Our life is never at a stand
> 'Tis like a fading flower,
> Death is always near at hand,
> Comes nearer every hour,
> Then let us all prepare to die
> Since death is near and sure,
> And then it will not signify
> If we were rich or poor.

Jane Hesketh's work   1843   Aged 11 years

Figure 3.1 A sampler. Samplers were commonly worked by young girls in the Victorian era

Also, I spotted a sampler in the museum in Southport's Botanic Gardens (Lancashire) worked at a similar time, and with the Bible as its source:

> Mary Ann Rimmer   Aged 12 years   1848
>
> Create in me a clean heart O God and
> Renew a right spirit within me.   Psalms.

In the Victorian period, great stress was also laid upon the child's knowledge of grammar, and a book published in 1878, which was lent to me recently, was written specifically for *young* children. Indeed, the preface states, 'This little book is meant for young children'. *Grammar For Beginners* by Dr Cornwell gives very comprehensive explanations,

EXAMPLES.—*He came to* ME. *He ran with* US.

EXPLANATION.—The words *me, us,* are in the Objective Case, governed by the Prepositions *to* and *with.* In the first sentence, we say, *He came to me,* not *to I,* because *me* is the Objective Case of *I,* and *to,* which is a Preposition, always has the Objective Case after it. In the second sentence, we say, *with us,* not *with we,* for *us* is the Objective Case of *we,* and *with,* which is a Preposition, always has the Objective Case after it.

79. RULE.—Prepositions govern the Objective Case ; as, *I sent a book to him.*

EXERCISE XXXV.

☞ (*a*) Point out the Objectives in the following sentences, and say why the words are in that Case :—

Diogenes lived in a tub. Saint Simon lived on a pillar. Charles the Fifth retired into a monastery. Mahomet pretended to see his visions in a cave away from all mankind. Charles the Twelfth of Sweden fled from Russia into Turkey, and was besieged in his house at Bender. York is on the Ouse, which is a river that runs into the Humber. The fir-tree grows in cold countries and on high mountains.

(*b*) Supply Pronouns in the Objective Case.

Give the penknife to (   ). My mamma told me to fetch a book for (   ). The book was not lost by (   ), but by (   ). You must go with (   ) if you can. The property belongs to (   ), and not to (   ).

Figure 3.2 An extract from *Grammar for Beginners* by Dr Cornwell, published specially for young children in 1878

examples and exercises in grammar ranging from nouns, pronouns, possessive pronouns, etc., to verbs (passive and active), tenses (past, present, future, conditional, subjunctive) and nominative, objective and dative cases. I have included above a brief exact from the book, since it illustrates how the objective case was taught.

There is a considerable amount of technical language in the explanations and the preface recommends that the examples and explanations be read over by the pupils and then discussed with the teacher before they are 'set on to learn' rules. The nature of the sentences in 'Exercise XXXV' illustrates the way in which grammatical knowledge was linked to the type of general knowledge which young children of the period were expected to learn. We see again in the sentence about York, the type of rote learning so prevalent at this time. It is interesting to note, too, that the exercises combine general knowledge with typical language of the period. Throughout the book there are considerable references *back* to grammar that has already been considered; thus the children were constantly revising their grammatical knowledge. I often feel that there is not always sufficient revision of work that has been done in some of our schools and adult education centres. It has seemed that some teachers and tutors have omitted revision of past work in their eagerness to proceed with new learning. However, Fred Schonell (1957, p. 20) regarded the revision of spellings as essential, stating: 'Weekly and monthly revisions, not necessarily by testing, consolidate progess made and repay initial expenditure of time and energy'. Similarly, Margaret Peters (1985) recommends the regular use of specially constructed dictation passages for revising spellings learned. Moreover, her many references to the effectiveness of systematic teaching implies that revision is an integral part of structured tuition.

Perhaps the requirements of the National Curriculum will provoke teachers into making careful revision of work learned an integral part of their lesson plans.

Education in the 1900s

It was not until 1899 that the school leaving age was raised from 10 to 12 years. However, the beginning of the twentieth century saw another great educational advance with the passing of the Balfour Act in 1902. This Act abolished the School Boards set up by the 1870 Education Act, replacing them with Local Education Authorities which were given power to provide secondary schools. At first, these schools charged fees, but they soon began to offer free places to a quarter of their intake.

Perhaps the greatest move forward in education in this century was the Hadow Report of 1931, which came to be regarded as a key statement of progressivism, stressing the importance of children's development, of learning through experience, and of a less authoritarian role for teachers. Thus, children began to be given some 'status' in the learning process and not regarded merely as receptacles for all kinds of facts learned by rote.

During the 1930s and 1940s, rote learning of multiplication tables and spellings was still evident in many schools, and though timetables were generally extending well beyond the 'three Rs' and religious instruction, to include, for example, history, geography, nature study and physical training, there were always *daily* periods devoted to arithmetic, spelling and dictation since a major concern was preparation for the scholarship examination (Goodfellow, 1988). (I can remember the rote and rhythmic learning of spelling; one of our class teachers was called Miss Phethean, and she was determined that we should all know how to spell her name correctly, thus we chanted P-H-E T-H-E A-N daily for the first week that we were in her class. I do not remember anyone forgetting it since we were all tested on it regularly!)

Handwriting was also usually considered to be important in any school's syllabus; often children were asked to copy out poetry, proverbs and letters to be taken home to parents, perhaps asking for contributions to a forthcoming 'bring and buy' sale in the school or to inform parents of school trips. The increasing use of duplicating machines and, more recently, photocopying machines, has meant that few schools require their children to write out information to be taken home. I feel it a pity that teachers do not utilise such occasions by encouraging children to write out the notes/letters. Like Margaret Peters, though, I do not think that such writing should be merely unthinking copying, letter by letter. Teachers could display the information to be communicated and discuss it, drawing children's attention to particular characteristics of the text (letter strings, etc.). In this way, teachers could help children to look 'with intent, interest . . . in a practical short-lived situation' (Peters, 1985, p. 52).

Fred Schonell

The extensive research of Fred Schonell resulted firstly from an investigation into disability in spelling among London elementary children. His book *Essentials in Teaching and Testing Spelling*, first published in 1932, was arguably the most commonly used textbook in schools during the 1950s. It has recently been revised by Pamela Wise (1985).

Words included in Schonell's lists were considered to be those required by children at varying ages and were based upon the written material of children aged from 7 to 12 years. He stated:

> The first essential is that children should be taught words which they use frequently in their written work and that they should not waste time learning words which they seldom use. (1957, p. 12)

The words were divided into six groups, each group representing the chronological age of the child. Thus, group 1 was designed for children aged 12 years. It is important to note Schonell's advice to teachers in his preface to the spelling lists (p. 10).

> Although the basis of both selection and grading has been
> frequency of child usage, yet in all cases, the lists should
> be sparingly supplemented with words of local significance,
> composition requirements and specific experiences.
> (1957, p. 10)

Schonell also stated:

> Use of a Group will vary considerably with the intellectual
> calibre of the class. (1957, p. 10)

It is my opinion that some teachers using Schonell's lists never actually read his recommendations for their use since teachers in schools that I visited as a student teacher and as a qualified teacher, appeared to work 'slavishly' and entirely from Schonell's list. It may well be that some teachers (and headteachers) disregard the author's instructions in the use of textbooks, workbooks, reading schemes, etc. Schonell recommended that teachers should introduce children to between three and five words per day; in the early stages of learning to spell, the words were fairly regular in terms of sound/symbol correspondence. For example:

GROUP I

Man	get	run
can	wet	gun
ran	let	sun
	met fun ant	
red	did	hot
bed	hid	not
fed	lid	blot
	spot led lip	
had	bud	tell
sad	mud	fell
glad	rug	bell
	dug well has	

Every three or four weeks, dictated passages could be given based on three or four sets of words. For example:

GROUP I
The man ran in the sun. He is so hot he has to get well.
He had to run and run. He fell by the well. The man is
glad to get wet (33 words).

Schonell found that four main types of grouping were useful. Firstly, he associated words of similar auditory and visual elements; these were illustrated in the previous examples from Group 1, and includes words such as power, shower, tower. In a second type of grouping, he associates words of similar visual, but slightly dissimilar auditory elements. For example:

stove
glove
prove

A third grouping combines words of common elements and contexts, as in:

needle   button
thimble   cotton

His fourth grouping includes words with common silent letters. For example:

knee   comb
kneel   crumb
knock   thumb
knob   climb

In the preface to his book, Schonell acknowledges the fact that some teachers consider spelling 'drill' as mechanical and disliked by children. However, he goes on to say that there is ample evidence that up to the age of about 9 years, rhythmic repetition is psychologically sound and goes on to quote Sir Percy Nunn (1930, p. 71):

. . . the child's repertoire of accomplishments is narrowly
limited, he loves, therefore, to repeat the familiar because
he gets from it the fullest sense of effective self-assertion.
(Schonell, 1957, p. 13)

Schonell also states:

> Defective pronunciation is a considerable source of
> misspelling, and a method of teaching which provides for
> repetition of common sound combinations, spoken as well
> as written, is making a dual contribution.
> (1957, pp. 16–17)

(Incorrect pronunciation will be referred to in the chapter on spelling
assessment.)

As has been stated already, Schonell was adversely criticised, especially
in the 1960s when it was considered that his teaching methods were based
only on the adults' views of words to be spelled at certain stages rather
than the child's actual needs. In fact, David Moseley stated:

> Future authors of spelling lists would do well to select their
> words not from adult vocabulary counts, but from the words
> actually used by children of different ages in free writing.
> (1974, p. 1)

However, as has been noted, Schonell did suggest that teachers using his
lists should select additional or alternative words which were appropriate to
their pupils; moreover, in preparing his lists, he took account of children's
needs at different stages and so a word such as 'downstairs' is in Group 2's
section, whereas 'envy' (a short, but less common word) is placed in Group
5 since it is likely to enter children's vocabulary at a later stage. A more
recent and (I think) valid criticism about spelling lists in general (not just
Schonell's) was made by Peters (1985); she considers that they do not
usually take account of the fact that children make considerable use of the
past tense and the plural form of words in the writing (though, there is *some*
evidence of the past tense on Schonell's Group 1 list, for example: ran,
did, hid, had). I also think that Schonell's dictation on page 33 warrants
comment. Clearly, the sentences are very contrived and do not form a
cohesive text. However, since the dictation is based upon the very
limited group of preceding words, it could be argued that the sentences
are discrete units of meaning. Admittedly though, 'He is so hot he has to
get well' is a very curious unit of meaning.

Apart from lists and dictations, Schonell also made several other
recommendations with respect to the teaching of spelling. For example,
he believed that homonyms and letter blends which sound alike should

be separated since confusion may occur if they are taught together. Thus *pear* and *pair* would appear in different lists, as would the digraphs (group of two letters representing one sound) *ou* and *ow*. From personal experience, I find that some teachers, parents and also volunteer tutors in ABE teach homophones together; in fact, I often hear *pair*, *pear* and *pare* discussed in one spelling session. Of course, children (and adults) who are good at spelling can cope with such instruction quite easily and, in any case, they often know these spellings already; it is the less able spellers who become confused by being overloaded by so much information about different word patterns and different word meanings. Indeed, Schonell constantly urged teachers to follow the maxim of 'a little and often' especially since his original lists were designed to help children with spelling difficulties.

It is interesting to note, too, that Schonell condemned teachers who divided words into syllables since, in his view, it distorted the actual pattern or schema of the word being learned (this view will be discussed in the chapters on teaching spelling). Like Peters (whose work we shall discuss shortly), he emphasised the visual rather than the aural aspect of words to be learned, though he also suggested that all channels of ingress be employed in learning (1957, p. 18), that is, visual, auditory, articulatory (correct pronunciation allowing for regional variations) and grapho-motor impressions (tracing words in the air or on a sand tray or desk).

Wise has made few changes to Schonell's spelling lists; in fact, the core of her spelling lists are in their original form. Her additions are 'new' words such as computer, television and video; they replace words such as oxen, grate, quart and wireless. Wise groups 'new' words according to Schonell's 'patterns' and categories. For example:

cheque	jeans
antique	anorak
mosque	sweater
plaque	trainers

Her revision of graded dictation passages for use in tests includes deletions of expressions such as: 'The Governor General of New Zealand'. However, many teachers do not consider class testing to be helpful, whether in the form of word tests or dictation tests, since they maintain that tests are damning for children who find spelling difficult, and serve merely to reinforce their feeling of failure. (Testing will be discussed in the chapters on teaching spelling.)

Despite criticisms of Schonell's work, I think that we should not overlook the many valuable elements of his philosophy. We should bear in mind that *regular* attention to spelling, related to words used frequently by the children, as well as words introduced by the teacher, will give prestige to the spellings within the writing process. Moreover, regular and brief instruction in which words are grouped with respect to similarity of constituent elements is far more likely to promote successful spelling and writing than lengthy but *occasional* 'bursts' of spelling instruction. As Schonell stated:

> The adult will see the fallacy of the latter procedure if he notes the accuracy and permanency of his recall in what for him is a comparable learning task, namely that of learning the spelling and meaning of sets of forty unfamiliar French or German words *en masse* at one presentation or in sections at several sittings. (1957, p. 17)

Margaret Peters

Margaret Peters was, until her retirement in the early 1980s, Tutor in Literacy at the Cambridge Institute of Education. She also worked as a primary school teacher, an educational psychologist, and a college of education lecturer. Her book, *Spelling: taught or caught?* was first published in 1967 and revised in 1985. Her doctoral research in the 1960s was concerned broadly with what the child brings to the skill of spelling and the extent to which teachers' attitudes to spelling affect the child's progress. Peters describes her research in *Success in Spelling* (1970).

It had become clear to Peters that 'favoured' children, that is, children from a home background in which adults were interested in language and learning and promoted it in their children, tended to spell without much difficulty. It became clear, too, that less 'favoured' children could also learn to spell without much difficulty provided that they were given good teaching. Peters qualified this statement, writing:

> Good teaching implies a rational, consistent systematic approach to the teaching of the skill. (1985, p. 14)

Peters' research also highlighted the fact that the children who learned to spell more easily tended to be those who had a high verbal intelligence.

However, the most important attribute they possessed was 'good visual perception of word forms' (1985, p. 24).

Since, in my opinion, Peters' two main observations regarding good teachers and good visual perception lie at the heart of helping children to become efficient spellers (and writers), I propose to consider some of her most important views/findings regarding the teaching of spelling.

She has always emphasised the differences between good and poor spellers, maintaining that good spellers are free to write with confidence and generally will attempt to spell words which are fairly new in their vocabulary. On the other hand, she states that poor spellers:

> . . . may write simply; they may avoid the words they use in everyday speech because they are too difficult to spell; they may not write at all. (1985, p. 7)

Peters emphasises, too, the differences between the spelling and the reading task and the fact that reading does not *necessarily* improve spelling since we do not look at every word that we read in detail. In fact, the better (and faster) reader pays only minimal attention to the structure of words read. She illustrates the point with the word *saucer* which may be read quite easily by junior children, especially if it is read in context. However, her research indicated that it was a very difficult word to spell (less than half of 988 year 5 children spelled it correctly), and it had 200 variations with regard to how it might have been spelled. For example: sauser (67 children), sorser (23 children) and suacer (23 children); less logical spellings included sud, sres and eswas (these latter spellings were given by individual children). It is interesting to note, too, that some very literate adults have no difficulty in *reading* words such as Czechoslovakia, diarrhoea, supersede, procedure, yet many of them may have difficulty in spelling those words correctly. As Peters says: 'It is special interest that makes one look carefully at a particular word' (1985, p. 16).

I recall a nurse who asked for my help in learning to spell 'diarrhoea'. She told me that only the latter part of the word caused difficulties, so when we noted that this consisted of *hoe* plus *a* success was practically guaranteed! This emphasises the need for novice spellers to look attentively and selectively at words to be learned. Like Schonell, Peters feels that children who are urged to 'say the word out loud, and write down what you hear' are generaly being taught a very unhelpful spelling method;

she gives examples of the words cup, done, does, blood and tough. The latter four words would be (and often are) spelled incorrectly if spelled according to sound.

Lanyon (1974, p. 23), however, acknowledges Peters' view, but maintains that some investigations support greater importance being given to auditory factors. He, for example, states that training in auditory discrimination and articulation of words (especially ones which are bi-syllabic) may help 8 to 10 year olds with their spelling. Similarly, Schonell (1957, p. 16) considers that defective pronunciation is a considerable source of misspelling. Though, like Peters, I consider that children's attention to the visual aspect is of great importance in spelling, there is no doubt that on occasions when children have to rely upon how they think a word sounds, plus their knowledge of letter strings, then mispronunciation of words may result in misspellings, for example: pation (patience); playgroung (playground); Normer (Norma). It thus seems that attention to the visual aspects of words should be accompanied by the teacher's *clear* pronunciation.

According to Peters, three main factors are generally present in successful spellers. These are:

- *verbal ability* (though Peters acknowledges that not all linguistically favoured children are good spellers);

- *visual perception and recall* (Peters states that deficits in this area may be compensated for by good teaching; children may be helped to an awareness of the generalisations which may be made about spelling patterns); and

- *perceptuo-motor ability* (Peters finds that there is a correlation between speedy, well-formed handwriting and good spelling).

With respect to the teaching of spelling, Peters has become known for the phrase 'caught or taught?' According to her, 'caught' means that spelling is picked up in certain favourable circumstances in the context of concerned and perceiving adults. She feels that 'catching' spelling may occur if parents and teachers direct children's attention (and especially very young children's) to the various spelling patterns, or as Peters says: 'serial probability within the spelling system' (1987, p. 178).

She explains how parents may, in addition to talking and reading to (and with) their children, not only point out the words they meet, but lightly and incidentally indicate the internal structure of the words. For example, the parent of a child called Martin may say: 'That bit's like a bit in your name' (as they look at Smarties or Mars Bars). Similarly, Peters maintains that the child who says: 'She's in me because she's Anna and I'm Joanna' has learned to look with interest at the internal structure of words and is catching spelling by becoming sensitised to spelling patterns. Moreover, Peters feels that parents who discuss the experiences of the day with pre-school children by reviewing them serially are helping to extend the children's imagery and serial span of apprehension, both important subskills for the child who is learning to 'catch' spelling. For example: 'First we went to Granny's . . . then we went to the supermarket' (1987, pp. 179–180).

Reception and nursery teachers may help by giving children pegs with their names on (not illustrations), and perhaps making some connection of words within words, for example 'Ti*moth*y collect *moths*'.

Peters' doctoral research indicates that carefulness evinced in the quality of handwriting is an important sub-skill of spelling. She goes on to say that carefulness in writing is significantly correlated with the speed of handwriting, and that casual and slow handwriting implies an uncertainty about letter formation and a time-consuming uncertainty about letter sequence as well as letter formation. Peters thus concludes that good handwriting is essential in the development of a competent speller and should be learned through identification, imitation and practice (1970, p. 74). She stresses the fact that a, o, d, g, q should all be formed by a counter-clockwise movement, and that vertical strokes of tall letters should begin at the top. (Chapter 6 considers handwriting and spelling.)

While agreeing in the main with Peters' view, I feel that the way many children are seated in classrooms (that is, often at tables in fours or sixes) may cause confusion during any directional instruction in handwriting since some children may have their backs or sides to the teacher or the blackboard. We shall see in the chapter on handwriting and spelling that it is recommended that instruction be given to small groups of children who are *facing* the teacher and/or blackboard, so that they may observe how teachers form letters and letter sequences and then imitate movements correctly. In several schools I have recently observed children who, because they are grouped 'socially' in fours and sixes, have to twist their bodies round continually in order to pay attention to instruction being given.

The use of personal dictionaries for each child is encouraged by Peters;

the teacher writes words required by the child for their written work in their personal dictionary. The child may then transfer the word/s to their work, but *not* by copying them.

As Peters says:

> . . . in order to exploit the visuo-motor nature of the spelling skill, it is important to teach children to look carefully at words and to write them without copying, for it is this strategy that helps the child to generalise from common letter sequences to new and previously unknown spellings. (1993, p. 180)

Peters recommends the 'Look – Cover – Write – Check' method (LC/WC) of transferring spellings to books. This method requires the child to:

1 *Look* carefully at the characteristics of the word to be transferred noting, in particular, any letter strings, then when it is thought that the word has been memorised;

2 *Cover* the word (with a paper or book etc) then;

3 *Write* the word/s in his or her work; and

4 *Check* that its spelling is correct by matching it with the word written by the teacher.

NB If the spelling/s are incorrect, the *whole* process should be repeated.

It is suggested by Peters that children should write in pencil so that any spelling errors may be rubbed out and written correctly in their work after carrying out the LC/WC process. This suggestion will be discussed further in the chapter on teaching spelling since I consider there is value in 'preserving' the initial misspelling (crossed out with one line of the pen or pencil) in order that the learner and the teacher may be aware of progress when previous misspellings are spelled correctly.

Like Schonell, Peters believes that regular spelling tests and dictations are essential in helping children to acquire automatic spelling skills. However, she suggests that spelling tests should be mainly 'self' tests in which children learn and test themselves (and/or each other) on selected words from their personal dictionaries. Similarly, dictations should be based upon work done by children so that spelling is not divorced from the writing process. Peters believes that dictations help to develop the children's sense of writing which flows. In 1975, her *Diagnostic and Remedial Spelling Manual* was published. This contains dictated passages as well as advice on how to analyse spelling errors. She believes that dictations which aim to help teachers to diagnose difficulties and assess progress should be of interest to the children for whom they are aimed. For example, a dictation passage for children aged 9–10 years begins: 'Late one night my friend woke me saying, "Would you enjoy a trial-run in my new helicopter?"'

More recently (1992) Margaret Peters and Brigid Smith have had a book published entitled *Spelling in context: strategies for teachers and learners*, which includes a photocopiable diagnostic grid for analysing children's spelling development, and also four diagnostic dictations which have been specially devised using word frequency data from children's own usage and which are graded in difficulty.

Also emphasised by Peters is the fact that any terms used by teachers for giving information about spelling should be clearly understood (and thus clearly explained), for example, when referring to tenses, vowels, consonants, doubling and blending. This is an area in which I am particularly interested; my studies in the early 1980s with children and adults suggested that teachers' explanations may be partially or even wholly misunderstood by some students and, what is even more important, both adults and children are often reluctant to admit that they have not understood (Mudd, 1987).

With respect to marking children's work, Peters suggests that teachers pick out the most important (to the child) misspellings and write them in the margin; and by their side should be written the part of the word which may be causing the confusion, for example, 'bought', *'ough'*. She observes that teachers (and parents) who themselves enjoy 'playing' with words and learning word derivations can generally inspire children with their enthusiasm:

> . . . the behaviour of the teacher determines, more than any other single factor, whether a child learns or does not learn to spell. (1985, p. 41)

In fact, Peters' doctoral research showed that after a period of two years, improvement in spelling occurred where 'rational and systematic teaching procedures' were employed (1970, p. 39). Conversely, in one school where there had been no list learning, no instruction and no testing, the children (with one exception) were, at the end of two years, making significantly more unreasonable than reasonable attempts at words they did not know.

Naturally, she is concerned about teachers who are rather diffident about teaching spelling, and lack knowledge about our language.

Peters recommends that books on spelling should show teachers *how* to help children to become aware of patterns of letter strings; she finds that many books which give lists of words to be used in spelling 'instruction' often give no information regarding teaching strategies. In fact, she and Charles Cripps (who has, like Peters, undertaken considerable research into the teaching of spelling, and whose views generally coincide with hers) found that only just over half of the authors reviewed by them (out of a total of 73) in *Appraisal of Current Spelling Material* (1982), presented a strategy for teaching children to spell. Peters' (1985) main ideas are encapsulated in the recommendations she made for teachers of spelling when she suggested that they should:

1   Teach systematically.

2   Use spelling lists from the children's work.

3   Give clear instruction on how to learn.

4   Give clear instruction on how to correct work (and this includes teaching children how to locate 'hard' spots). By such instruction, novice learners become responsible for their own learning.

5   Encourage a correctly formed style of handwriting.

Joyce Todd is a class teacher who undertook research into the teaching of spelling. Her book *Learning to Spell: A Resource Book for Teachers* (1982) examines the way that children learn to spell and outlines many activities which are likely to help teachers. She states on p. viii: 'children learn best when they are directing and discovering their learning'. In addition, Todd's book puts forward many views held by Schonell and Peters. Like them, she feels that a child's early years are vital in sowing the seeds of, and interest in, spelling; it is in his or her early years that a child acquires good or bad habits. Also, she urges teachers to emphasise the visual rather than the auditory aspects of words to be learned. She points out further that children's first words are generally not regular in terms of symbol/sound correspondence (for example, their own names and words such as you, was, me, my), thus the sounding out of such words would be likely to result in misspellings (in fact, most children are taught these words as 'sight words'). Todd goes on to say that children should be made aware very early in their school life of the reasons *why* they should not rely on auditory analysis in the spelling process. Similarly, Albrow (1974) suggests that we do not teach letters as 'static' but as having many 'jobs' to do, for example: fruit/boot, guard/yard. However, Todd also considers that knowledge about letter sounds and names, and knowledge about letter strings, is essential in both reading and writing. This knowledge is vital in establishing the *first* letter(s) in words to be read or written. Unlike Schonell, Todd thinks that splitting up words into syllables may be useful in helping learners to remember their spellings, but she warns against putting in lines to separate the syllables since these distort the *whole* image of the word. Also, Lanyon (1974, referred to on page 38 suggests that teachers who articulate bi- or multi-syllabic words carefully are helping to improve children's auditory discrimination, their articulation of words and possibly their spelling. I think it was the *division* of words by lines to which Schonell objected when he argued against splitting words into syllables.

Todd's book also gives some practical guides regarding how teachers may help children to become effective and speedy users of dictionaries (this will be discussed in the chapter on teaching spelling). There is a danger in teachers giving only one or two class lessons in dictionary use and assuming that that is all the child requires in order to be able to locate words quickly.

Like Peters, Todd stresses the importance of the child becoming responsible for his or her own learning and getting into a routine of self-checking written work, using, among other resources, dictionaries and personal word books to do this. Progress in spelling is, she believes (like Schonell and Peters), marked by regular testing; however, she believes that tests should cater for differing spelling abilities within a class. (This will be discussed in the chapters on spelling instruction.)

A major concern of both Todd and Peters is the fact that many teachers themselves need education regarding the spelling process. Todd feels that teachers' lack of confidence in their own spelling abilities seems to result in them either working totally from rule books and lists, or viewing the teaching of spelling in a rather *arbitrary* manner, and with little remedial help for those with spelling difficulties. Indeed, both Todd and Peters agree that teachers' positive attitudes to spelling and language often correlate highly with children who are interested in particular in accuracy in their spelling, and in language in general, and who write with confidence.

It has been noted that Schonell, Peters and Todd all state that, in order to become efficient spellers, children should concentrate on the visual aspects of print. Peters' research findings certainly support this view. She summarises her conclusions formed as a result of her investigations regarding important factors which contribute to success in the skill of spelling:

> The skill depends on an individual's habitual perceiving in large units of common letter sequences, and retaining these, which may not necessarily be dependent on meaningful words, but which are in a probability order of occurrence in a particular language. Until this becomes automatized, utilization of these is a priority strategy. Other strategies such as auditory/articulatory, phoneme encoding into graphemes, are available, but less effective. (1970, p. 76)

To illustrate this point, Peters refers to two children aged 11, one spelled 'enthusiasm' as 'imfuasem', the other spelled it as 'infuseasumn'. Peters comments that both spellings derive from auditory or articulatory faults but, in the latter example, both 'in' and 'fuse' are quite reasonable alternatives, and the final syllable clearly reflects the final syllable of words such as 'autumn'.

Phonological aspects of spelling

On the other hand, the research of Usha Goswami and Peter Bryant (1990) stresses how children's earliest attempts at writing show how they utilise knowledge about sound/symbol correspondence, reflecting their great sensitivity to the sounds of our language. They observe:

> Experiments on connections between children's awareness of sound and their progress in reading and spelling have been remarkable. (1990, p. vii)

In the final chapter of their book, they put forward their own developmental theory for reading and spelling, maintaining that it is not a theory about stages, but a theory which 'concentrates on causal connections' (1990, p. 146). They consider three main causal factors in the development of reading and spelling. Firstly, they refer to children's

sensitivity to sounds in words long before they learn to read, and this includes sensitivity to rhyme (or as they say rime) and onset (words which begin with similar sounds as in alliteration). Many very young children are able to produce rhyme, for example, David (who is referred to on page 54, figure 4.2) could not read or write, but was able to make up a rhyme which he said orally many times.

> When it's Easter, let's have measter
> When it's spring, let's sit on a swing.

The rhyme also evidences rhythm and repetition. Similarly, Cathy (who is referred to on page 74, figure 5.6) made up alliterative nonsense jingles at the age of 3 years, for example:

> Bim, Bam, Bom – Bing, Bang, Bong

Note again the repetition and rhythm in the jingle.

Goswami and Bryant consider that children who become adept at recognising common rimes and onsets are generally able to:

> . . . form categories of words and when they begin to read
> they recognise that words in the same categories often have
> spelling patterns in common. (1990, p. 147)

Secondly, they maintain that the experience of coming to grips with alphabetic script has an enormous effect on children's awareness of sounds. They stress the teaching aspect of this knowledge, rather than its incidental acquisition:

> . . . there is no doubt that for children of five and six
> years of age, the experience of being taught to read and
> spell is an extremely effective way to learn about
> phonemes. (1990, p. 148)

Children's knowledge about phonemes is obvious in much of their early writing, as we shall see in Chapters 4 and 5. However, Goswami and Bryant find it ironic that children do not always use this phonemic knowledge in their early reading; this will be discussed shortly when we consider some of the work of Peter Bryant and Lynette Bradley.

Goswami and Bryant's third causal link is really a qualitative change which occurs roughly after two years' experience of learning to read. Up to this time, it seems that children seldom make connections between reading and spelling, and they carry them out in different ways (as we shall see when reference is made to Bryant and Bradley's research). After about two years, however, children generally begin to connect reading and spelling, and they become readier to use their knowledge about sounds in their reading as well as their spelling. It should be noted, though, that Goswami and Bryant state with respect to the third causal link: 'We have to admit that this idea is still speculative' (1990, p. 149).

Research undertaken by Byrant and Bradley with children who find reading difficult and 'normal' readers in 1978 (and published in 1980) considers the puzzle of why children sometimes can write words which they cannot read. They believe (like Goswami and Bryant) that the solution to the puzzle lies in the fact that reading and spelling are tackled by children in very different ways; their observations of children spelling words showed that they would often use a phonological strategy quite explicitly.

> If we asked them to write down the word 'bun' they would often say b-u-n aloud whilst they wrote. (1980, p. 362)

Interestingly, they found in their research that many children in both reading ability groups spelled more words correctly than they read correctly, and this applied to six words in particular: *bad, fit, slid, upset, cot, sunlit.* The researchers commented that these particular words are probably easier from a phonological point of view because most do not contain any consonants blended within a syllable (*slid* seems to be the exception). Conversely, the words that were found to be spelled incorrectly most often were those with consonant clusters (for example, *pretended*). Various other experiments had similar findings. Among final comments made by the authors is the fact that children may be helped (or as they say 'pushed', 1980, p. 368) into reading words which they have spelled by being persuaded to adopt a phonological strategy in their reading as well as in their spelling for words which are visually unfamiliar to them. This comment also implies that Goswami's and Bryant's third causal link in the development of reading and spelling, whereby children see the connection between reading and spelling, may be promoted by explicit teacher instruction. (The research of Goswami and Bryant, and Bradley and Bryant, will be referred to further in Chapters 4 and 9.)

Similarly, Temple *et al.* (1988) in *The Beginnings of Writing* (2nd edn) stress novice writers' attention to what they hear as they write. They observe that spellings which young children produce on their own follow the rule that letters talk:

> Any letter that a child puts into a word is intended to represent sound. (1988, p. 56)

They go on to point out that when children spell what they hear, some sounds are overshadowed by others and not heard distinctly. These observations are exemplified in Emma's work (page 74, figure 5.6) as she writes:

> gt wl lv Emma (Get well, love Emma).

Interestingly, though such spellings are commonly referred to as invented spellings (and will be discussed in Chapter 4), Temple *et al.* argue that spellings such as 'wrrx' (works) and 'haws' (house) are so strange to the eye, it is safe to conclude that the children are not imitating anyone else or dimly remembering a standard spelling, and in this sense are invented. Yet the children do employ consonants to represent their standard sound value, and so the children must have learned something about spelling from someone outside of themselves; in this sense these relationships are not invented (1988, p. 56).

It seems that Temple *et al.*, like Goswami and Bryant, and Bryant and Bradley, are stressing the importance of teaching and learning (albeit quite informal) in the earliest stages of becoming literate.

In their book, Temple *et al.* also discuss how we make speech sounds. They note that breath and vocal bands do not give us speech, it is the shaping activity of the tongue, lips, teeth, mouth and nasal passages which work together to form speech sounds. Then, for example, they ask the reader to make the consonants b-g-d; all of these are alike in the manner in which they are made in that they stop the air flow, and in linguistic terms are called *stops*. Among other consonants are the fricatives such as s-z-v-f-th (as in *then* and as in *thin*). These sounds are made by the friction (or restriction) of breath in a narrow opening. The point being made is that many sounds are alike in the place and manner that they are made; it is the voicing which is different. Temple *et al.* go on to say that if a child wants to represent a sound in spelling a word, but cannot find a perfect fit, it chooses a near fit, a letter name that is somewhat like the sound it wants to represent. This may account for what may seem to us strange choices of letters to represent sounds in children's spellings. We see this, for example, in the work of the child who wrote 'tey' (they) and 'fings' (things) in figure 5.9 on page 77. Note that we make the sound 't' by placing the tongue very close to the space where 'th' is made. Like Bryant and Bradley, Temple *et al.* observe the explicit and often exaggerated way in which young children often produce speech sounds as they write, and they comment that the child is 'exploring place, manner and voicing' (1988, p. 64).

It seems then that teachers and parents may help children to articulate words correctly and thus raise their awareness of how particular sounds are formed/voiced. In fact, both Schonell and Peters have referred to spelling errors which result from children's misarticulations of words well beyond the age of 7 years. Temple *et al.* refer also to some of the difficulties which our spelling system often causes for novice spellers; not least is the fact that our 26 letters of the alphabet have 44 sounds. Included in the difficulties to which they refer are digraphs such as ch, sh, th, ph; the idea that two letters can represent one sound is not easy for a beginning writer. Also referred to by the authors is the fact that short vowels (as in p**a**t, p**e**t, p**i**t, p**o**t, p**u**t) often cause problems for young writers. This is because, in construction, vowels are not very different from each other; the authors explain:

> We make vowels by holding the tongue in certain positions
> as voiced air passes through the mouth. (1988, p. 69)

Morphemic endings, such as the past tense marker -*ed* may also cause problems for the novice writer (a morpheme is a meaningful unit of language) since it has three pronunciations: -d, -t and -id (as in mov*ed*, dropp*ed*, buri*ed*). It is then pointed out by Temple *et al.* that though not all children use invented spellings, those who do use them are acting mostly upon their intuitions. They go on to suggest that later spelling goes through a transitional stage in which children will be influenced generally by their increasing progress in the reading process and by teachers' instruction.

The authors then consider again what they call an 'early phonemic speller', and among the many strategies suggested for promoting their spelling skills we find that reading to the children by adults plays a major part. It is, for example, suggested that adults should read aloud to a child as the child sits on the adult's lap; the latter should direct the child's attention to a word at exactly the instant the word is read aloud. By this means, the child is being introduced to the connections between the printed and the spoken word, the concept of a word, the left to right sequence of print, etc. It is also suggested that children's written work at this stage should be accepted for what it is by both parents and teachers, with both teachers and parents understanding the value of encouragement, practice and freedom to make errors in learning to spell. Similarly, as the novice writer moves on to 'letter-name' spelling, teachers and parents are encouraged to talk about the content of the child's writing, and not to focus attention on spellings. (In the next chapter we shall see that even after year 3, Donald Graves pays attention firstly to *what* the child writes and secondly to *how* he or she writes.)

From this stage onwards, Temple *et al.* believe that children need to be led gradually to learn patterns at work in standard spelling, they state:

> . . . it is best if they learn these in the context of meaningful writing, though isolated activities are sometimes helpful. (1988, p. 114)

Like Peters, the authors also refer to the part that memory plays in learning to spell as well as 'a mind for learning' about how words come to be spelled the way they are, and how they resemble and differ from other words.

> The memory thrives on associations: reasoning and reflecting on spellings thus makes memorization easier. (1988, p. 116)

We have then, on the one hand, Schonell, Peters and Todd who stress the importance of the development of children's visual perceptions in order that they may become effective spellers. Peters does though acknowledge spelling strategies related to what the child hears but, as we have seen, maintains that the latter strategies are *less* effective in helping them to become competent spellers.

On the other hand, the studies of Goswami and Bryant, and Bryant and Bradley, indicate that there is a strong connection between children's spelling (and reading) and their phonological skills. Yet, the former researchers also acknowledge that:

> . . . it is impossible to spell English properly just on the basis of letter-sound relationships. No one who relies just on a

> phonological code will ever spell 'laugh', 'ache', or even 'have' properly. (1990, p. 53)

It is my belief that both viewpoints are important as we help children to learn to spell (and read), and that, moreover, the main findings and recommendations of Temple *et al.* encapsulate the main thrust of both arguments. Thus, the importance of what the child hears in his or her earliest writing attempts is acknowledged, plus the fact that in the earliest stages of literacy, children need to be introduced to how our sound/symbol relationship works, with plenty of pre-school reading with adults, informal experience in letter sounds and names and alliteration and rhyme. Such experience should generally help them to take their first steps in reading and communicating their thoughts/ideas in writing (albeit their spelling is not always conventional). However, once these first steps have been taken, there should be a cross-fertilisation of methods, so that gradually children realise there are options in our language. Thus, though they may hear the rhyme in *new* and *blue* and the alliteration in *kill* and *can*, they should, bit by bit, be helped to look too at the visual aspects of words with care, noting the visual differences as well as the auditory similarities.

If we do not help children to make this transition, they may continue to spell as the boy of 14 did when he wrote about the 'noow pawsh' (see page 2).

We shall see in Chapters 7, 8 and 9 that attention is given to phonological, articulatory and visual aspects of the skill of spelling so that they all play interactive parts in helping the novice writer to become more competent. As children progress in this competence, though, attention to the visual aspects of spelling will gradually become more dominant. This visual dominance is vital in a language which is spelled (as we saw in Chapter 2) roughly the way it sounded about five hundred years ago!

In summary then, the main concerns of researchers into the effective teaching of (and preparation for) spelling and writing include:

- plenty of early (pre-school) child/adult reading and informal 'literacy', games and discussions which include words, letter names and sounds, onset and rime;

- a positive teacher attitude, which in turn may be reflected in the children's attitudes;

- clear articulation of words studied;

- helping children to pay attention to the visual structure of words;

- helping children to memorise word patterns and avoid copying;
- studies of common letter patterns;
- studies of less common letter patterns;
- regular but brief periods of instruction;
- regular, brief and informal tests on words studied – preferably in a meaningful context;
- handwriting instruction which encourages a flowing style and correct letter formation;
- studies of origins of words and word relationships (in terms of meaning);
- encouragement of children's responsibility for their own learning.

NB Whenever possible, spellings which are studied should be relevant to the children's needs; and needs will differ according to their stage of development in the writing process.

Summary

This chapter has considered some of the main teaching methods in the nineteenth century, and it has also given particular attention to the practical teaching methods suggested by Schonell and Peters in the twentieth century. Underlying their views on spelling is the fact that it should be studied as part of the writing process. Schonell's lists were based upon children's continuous writing, and as Peters says:

> Spelling is of no more use intrinsically than hopping or adding. Spelling is no use unless one wants to write, but to write without being able to spell would be to court circumlocution, to fail to express what one has to say with precision and to fail in fact to communicate. (1970, p. 77)

It is thus intended in the next chapter to consider the writing process as a whole, beginning with children's early attempts and moving on to some of the ideas currently put forward for developing/extending children's writing.

4 Spelling within the writing process

We have already seen that spelling researchers such as Schonell (1942) and Peters (1985) state most emphatically that spelling should be embedded in the writing process and not merely a study of words and letters in isolation, unrelated to general class work or the children's needs. It seems relevant, therefore, to discuss current views on developing and extending children's writing as a whole; we shall begin with children's *earliest* attempts to communicate in print, attempts which reveal their initiative in inventing symbols to represent meaningful communication.

Invented spelling

Children's first 'writings' clearly illustrate their knowledge of the purpose of the writing process as evidenced by the pre-school child, Kelly, aged 4 years (see figure 4.1). She has made an attempt to copy the date from an adult, but her 'writing' about the paddling pool is all her own work. It is interesting to note the joined nature of her scribbles; Cripps and Cox (1990) remark upon the nature of children's scribbles, and use it as one of the reasons for teaching joined writing to reception children rather than print. Moreover, children's early scripts often demonstrate that they do not differentiate between letters, squiggles and numbers as they 'write'; nevertheless, the message may be quite clear to the child. (See figure 4.2 in which David, aged 5 years, writes a birthday wish to his father.) As Hall says (1987, p. vii)

> . . . children observe and think about many features of the world, so they look at and reflect upon literate acts . . . Most children will arrive at school knowing something about what written language is, how it works and what it is used for.

I think that the key words in the preceding quotation are 'most' and 'something' since we shall see that researchers such as Linnea Ehri (1991) consider that most children need explicit instruction regarding sounds and symbols if they are to make *progress* in writing (and reading).

52

Figure 4.1   First 'writings' by Kelly, aged 4 years

Anne Robinson (1988, p. 102) similarly describes how young children's first unaided 'writing' is meaningful to them; she refers to Justin, aged 5 years, who was puzzled when he tried to read back his own story (the 'story' about 'Jaws' consisted of about 60 letters printed randomly). Robinson states that though he had letter/sound knowledge, he did not reflect it in his writing; it seemed that though he realised that reading could make use of this knowledge, he had not transferred this knowledge to the writing process. To him (and to David in figure 4.2) writing was simply related to producing recalled visual shapes. Robinson also refers to a child, Robert, aged 5 years and 1 month (p. 103). He had progressed further and wrote, 'n.f.w.a.f.a.l.p.a.n.p' (his oral translation of his writing was 'N fireengine with a fire and lots of people and 'n dog'. As Robinson observes, he is clearly using critical letters to symbolise words, with the dots showing where the words are. Robinson observes too that many children assume that letters represent words since teachers are frequently heard saying 'A is for apple' or 'B is for ball'. (We shall see later in this chapter though that Goswami and Bryant (1990) consider young children's use of letters to represent words to be a symptom of an early

Figure 4.2 Children's early writing often doesn't discriminate between letters, numbers and squiggles

phonological stage.)

A stage further is illustrated by an older child aged 8 years with learning difficulties. This child, though behind in terms of development, is nevertheless progressing in terms of expressing ideas in writing which may be relatively easily understood (see figure 4.3).

Here we see a mixture of words which have been memorised (I - am - my - the) interspersed with words which mainly reflect beginnings and ends of words; also the child has constructed something recognisable as a sentence. ('Today is Monday' was, of course, copied from the teacher's writing.)

Amusing examples of children's invented spellings (and initiative) are illustrated by Bissex (1980, p. 3). She wrote about her son, Paul (aged 5 years), who, being unable to distract her from reading, used some rubber letter stamps to print the message: 'RUDF' (Are you deaf?). Paul was a prolific writer and his writing tended to be purposeful as is exemplified

Figure 4.3 Despite learning difficulties, this child's writing may be relatively easily understood

by: 'DO NOT DSTRB GNYS AT WRK' (Do not disturb. Genius at work). Clearly his writing purposes differed from those given by the 5-year-old child in Newcastle who, when asked why people wrote, replied: 'Writing helps us to learn. Learn to write for your own health, Mrs Adde and God' (Czerniewska, 1989, p. 60). Czerniewska also referred to a young Indian girl's writing in which she showed her awareness of what texts look like (to her) and also her knowledge of how English and Urdu are written, since her 'text' included letter shapes which were based on English letter shapes randomly interspersed with Urdu writing patterns (p. 58). Similarly, she referred to a nursery teacher who put up musical notations on the classroom walls and received 'writing' from his children which reflected musical notation, shapes, numbers and letters. These examples indicate the extent to which children's environment can influence their thinking and their writing. Hall (1987) is therefore critical of schools which do not provide an environment in which children can participate in a variety of purposeful activities. Indeed, he considers that children's pre-school experiences are generally far richer (in terms of literacy development and awareness) than those in school. He refers to Juleibo's (1985) study of five Canadian children's experiences at home and in kindergarten. She found that many of the stimulating conditions under which literacy was emerging at home, 'disappear at school, even at "pre-school" level' (Hall, p. 75).

However, the idea of children becoming able to identify print in their environment, which subsequently provides them with the foundation for learning about the graphic system, has been challenged by Ehri (and others). Ehri maintains that to begin processing graphic cues to read words, children must acquire certain prerequisites, such as letter knowledge and phoneme awareness, and that pre-readers who lack such knowledge may appear to read signs in their environment, but they are 'reading' the environment, not the print (1991, p. 61).

While agreeing with the view that school should provide children with an environment which gives high status to literacy, and that teachers should be seen to give status to literacy by themselves engaging in reading and writing in the classroom, I consider that comparisons between homes (and especially homes in which literacy is given status) and school will generally highlight the richness of stimulation that may be given by parents to one (or more) children. We should not forget (as Hall also acknowledges) that teachers are usually working with large numbers of children of widely differing backgrounds and literacy levels; though it is fairly easy for infant teachers to provide a stimulating environment in which all the children are busily involved in working individually or in small groups, it requires an experienced and very perceptive teacher to ensure that all the children are progressing in their literacy experiences, and that those with difficulties are being detected *and* given appropriate help (that is, 'window dressed' classrooms are not enough; it is the quality of the teaching that counts).

Like Hall, Anne Robinson (1988) feels that teachers should provide a wide range of stimulating literacy experiences for young children, and she is critical of reception teachers who simply require children to write over and under the teacher's writing, or to copy from the board, or work cards without giving them opportunities to write unaided and thus take responsibility for their own work. She realises that 'To be faced with writing in the "raw", with marks and spellings which to the unpractised eye seem bizarre, can be very disturbing for adults' (1988, p. 98).

Indeed, Goswami and Bryant (1990, p. 51) think that children's invented spellings reflect their own awareness of sounds, which in some ways is different, and strictly speaking, a more accurate representation than an adult's. Moreover, they suggest that a 6-year-old girl who writes 'Tom nicta cr' (Tom nicked a car) gives a better phonological representation of the sounds of the words 'nicked a' than does the traditional spelling whereby the letters 'ed' are sounded as 't'. They comment, too, on the two-letter spelling of car, stating that because young children know the names of alphabetical letters as well as the sounds (alphabetical names are often learned *before* their sounds), there is frequent confusion regarding letters such as 'r' (whose alphabetical name is 'ar'). Similarly, the child referred to by Bissex (1980) was clearly using his knowledge of letter names when he wrote 'RUDF' to his mother. Among other potentially confusing letter names are: ef (F), el (L) and em (M) which may result in 'wl' for 'well' (see figure 5.6 on page 74), 'ma' for 'Emma' and 'ptr' for 'Peter'.

Goswami and Bryant refer too to Charles Read's (1986) book *Children's Creative Spelling*. (It was Read who, in the early 1970s, pointed out the significance of children's invented spelling.) One of the most consistent examples of children's early spellings showing an awareness of phonetic distinctions is in Read's finding that children frequently write 'chr' at the beginning of syllables starting with a 'tr' in conventional spelling. For example, 'chribls' may be written for 'troubles', 'chruc' for 'truck' or 'aschray' for 'ashtray'. Read explains this:

> . . . the /t/ of "trip" is not the same as the /t/ of 'tip'. It is affricated . . . like the sound in "chip" which is essentially /t/ plus /s/ (sh). (p. 20)

A delightful example of a child hearing 'ch' in words was evidenced when a 7-year-old girl wrote to me about the 'tchoolipps' in her garden. Interestingly, as adults, *we* may need to use phonic strategies to identify the word as 'tulips'. Young children (and in my experience, novice adult writers too) can represent a phonetic distinction which most adult writers have long ceased to notice because they know so much about spelling.

It seems that just as Goodman's (1973) work on miscue analysis in reading gave teachers an insight into children's knowledge of the reading process and their reading strategies (via their uninterrupted oral, taped readings of passages), so teachers can obtain valuable information about children's understanding of the writing process by studying their unaided writing. Margaret Peters (1993, pp. 182–3) refers to the developmental stages which children pass through in their spelling. These stages move from rudimentary letter formation, with little or no knowledge of letter sound correspondence, through the stage when letters are written according to sound (phonetic stage) to the point where the child moves on from sound to visual appearance and is applying a rudimentary knowledge of spelling patterns. Goswami and Bryant, though, believe that:

> . . . a great deal of the development takes the form of children just getting gradually better at strategies which they use right from the start. (1990, p. 147)

Nevertheless, the more that teachers know about children's spelling development, the more they will be able to assess children's progress and supply remediation where necessary. While agreeing with the value of teachers being able to use children's unaided spelling as a tool for diagnosing difficulties and assessing progress (and this will be discussed in the chapter on the assessment of spelling progress), I feel that copying, too, has value in providing the novice writer with models of the writing process and, particularly, copying which is accompanied by teachers 'talking aloud' about the work to be copied, for example, letter formation and the use and purpose of capitals and full stops. Reading aloud (by teachers) of the work to be copied is valuable, too, as it provides a language experience for the children which is also seen in print. After all, teachers and most parents recognise the great value of reading aloud to children (particularly with expression) and thus providing a model for the reading process (see Meek (1982) and Perera (1984)).

We see then that young children may develop as writers through their own observations at home, in school and in their world in general, but this needs to be accompanied by explicit instruction from parents and teachers. However, as has been stated many times (and I feel that it cannot be overstated) spelling should be developed within the writing process; and since the National Curriculum recommends that after levels one and two in writing (in which children are concerned mainly in writing accounts of personal experiences and making up or recalling stories), they should have frequent opportunities to write in different contexts and for a variety of purposes and audiences, including themselves, it seems relevant to refer briefly to authors who have written about developing children's writing. Thus, Donald Graves' and Roger Beard's main views on this subject will be considered.

Developing children's writing

Donald Graves

Graves' (1975) original study was based on only four classes of children in a middle-class community and thus some critics have suggested that his (1983) book is more like 'reportage' than a research-based study (see Beard, 1993, pp. 2–3). However, I consider that there is considerable value in many of the suggestions which Graves puts forward. In *Teachers and Children at Work* (1983), Graves' emphasis is on the teacher and the child working together to write; he feels that the tone is set by what the teacher does, not what the teacher says (p. 12). Thus, discussing, planning and sharing writing is vital, with teachers planning *their* writing quietly while the children do the same; alternatively, teachers may plan their written work in front of the class on overhead projectors (OHPs) or large sheets of paper, talking as they write about their aims and plans and any areas of difficulty. Graves further recommends that both teachers and children write about what they know, and that children be allowed to choose a subject to write about rather than the teacher choosing it for them. There are, of course, many occasions when all of us need some inspiration to write, and this certainly applies to many children. This is where teachers may use their expertise to promote discussion and thinking about some topic of interest which may be later used as a basis for developing children's writing.

According to Graves, rules form an integral part of writing sessions, and any rules should be clearly understood by all the children. For example, there should be no interruptions during writing periods, and children should know where pens, paper, folders are and what to do when work is finished without the perpetual 'where, what, when' type of questions – especially when teachers are working with other children (or, to use Graves' expression 'in conference'). It should be noted that Graves assumes the whole class will be engaged in writing as opposed to working on a variety of subjects, as is common practice in schools which have integrated day organisation. (Interestingly, the DES report on *Curriculum Organisation and Classroom Practice in Primary Schools* by Robin Alexander, Jim Rose and Chris Woodhead (1992, p. 28), generally supports the view that whole class teaching provides order, control, purpose and concentration.)

After the planning stage, Graves suggests that teachers move round the children to discuss their writing, but this is not haphazard, a record of the children should be kept, so that, for example, in a lesson of 40 minutes perhaps six children will have been given help individually. He also recommends that writing experiences should occur daily or at least four times per week, thus it is possible to see a class of 30 children at least once per week. This means that no children are being overlooked, especially those experiencing difficulties. Graves maintains that writing taught once or twice a week is just enough to remind 'weaker' writers that they cannot write, and teachers that they cannot teach (p. 90).

While discussing children's work, Graves puts the stress on the child, with the child talking about the writing, reading it, and perhaps expanding on it after open-ended questions by the teacher. Since the content of the work is thereby given status, this method would seem to help overcome the view held by many children that writing is judged to be good by teachers if it is neat, correctly spelled and long!

Graves also suggests that if children cannot use punctuation effectively, teachers may put it in and ask children to read it *and* obey the punctuation marks so that they may become aware of punctuation's function of helping readers to understand texts more easily. (I find that an amazingly large number of adults, including teachers, still define full stops as being required in order to give the reader time to take breaths; it seems that this idea is being passed on to pupils since it is so widely held.)

As with writing sessions, Graves believes that spelling instruction should be regular; he thinks that instruction once a week is virtually useless. He suggests that brief, daily spelling instruction gives the teacher access to discuss spelling in the context of the children's work. However, he does not clarify whether or not instruction is with the *whole* class in relation to the work of one or more children, or whether it is with individuals or small groups. Unlike Peters (1985), he dissuades children from rubbing out errors, he believes (as I do) that they are valuable in marking progress and difficulties.

Like many teachers, Graves publishes children's work; he allows children to select their 'best' work from their folders. Integral in his methodology is the encouragement of children to assess their own work. Before publication, spelling (and other) errors are corrected as children re-read and re-draft their work. If children do not 'spot' errors (of any kind), Graves suggests that teachers may say something like: 'There are four more spelling mistakes in your work. Also, you have missed out a question mark. Can you identify them?' Again, we see that content has been given the first emphasis; correct spelling, grammar, punctuation are

requisites of the writing process when the writing is to be published and/
or displayed.

As stated earlier, Graves places great importance on recording children's
progress and difficulties and suggests that the children too see the record of
their progress, perhaps inside the back cover of their folders. This might
include information about use of: capitals, quotation marks, full stops,
question and exclamation marks, possessive apostrophes and the ability
to proof-read for grammatical and spelling errors. (I think that
information about the nature of the child's published/displayed work could
be included in the folder, thus giving emphasis to the finished products.)
Moreover, Graves firmly believes that children who are successful writers
work in an environment where literature and poetry play a prominent part.
He further considers that some rote learning of parts of poems or stories
and the copying of some poetry is essential in providing models upon which
children may base their own writing.

Generally, Graves' recommendations/advice to teachers is somewhat
didactic in its nature, and though in particular his 'rules' for writing
sessions may seem at variance with the 'free' atmosphere in some
classrooms, I consider that Graves' methods balance more formal and
structured classroom organisation with teaching methods which allow for
the development of the individual child. For example, there has been a recent
trend in encouraging children to re-draft *all* pieces of written work; Graves,
however, suggests that children take responsibility for omitting 'less
good' work from their folders, and in such cases no re-drafting is
undertaken. Overall, Graves' suggestions encourage children to become
more involved in, and responsible for, their written work in a classroom
which is conducive to thought and private discussions.

NB In the chapter on teaching spelling at Key Stage 2 (see page 138), three
consecutive lessons will be outlined in which the author worked with children
aged 8–9 years. The lessons combined discussion, poetry, spelling and
writing. Many of Graves' ideas were incorporated in the lessons and adjusted
to suit the children (and the author).

Roger Beard

In *Children's Writing in the Primary School* (1984), Beard, like Graves,
considers that exposure to literature and poetry is likely to have a positive
effect on children's written work. He goes on to suggest that 'quality'
authors should receive a much higher profile (in fact, Beard's first page
shows the writing of a 9-year-old child who was greatly influenced by

hearing the beginning of Dylan Thomas's *Under Milk Wood*.) Similarly, while I am in favour of 'coaxing' children to an appreciation of written and spoken language via, for example, writers like Roald Dahl, whose humour usually appeals to children immediately, I feel that there should be a balance of the popular and the classic in literary experiences.

Again, like Graves, Beard considers that the development of planning, composing and reviewing activities in the writing process needs far more attention; it seems that all too often children are simply requested to write from 'cold' and then teachers simply react to the end product, often concerning themselves firstly with spelling errors. He also agrees that teachers need to be seen writing and states that:

> Far more is likely to be gained from the teacher attempting writing which has something of a challenge in it, a haiku poem, an amusing anecdote, or a polite letter of complaint to a touchy neighbour, with the teacher thinking aloud in front of groups of children as the writing is composed and written on a surface where they can easily follow the words as they appear. (1989, p. 144)

I have carried out similar activities with student teachers and assumed the role of teacher with the students taking on the role of children. The 'children' gave me a choice of three subjects from which I chose one, so that I could not be accused of having previously prepared for the writing experience! Using the OHP, I then talked aloud while jotting down the outline/plan of my proposed writing. Subjects suggested included: recollections of Christmas, litter, my favourite hobby. Also, some students asked me to attempt a limerick using any student's name. The 'jotting' session was followed by consideration of the sequence of the items in the outline, sometimes resulting in the deletions or additons to the original plan. I must admit that when I first undertook such 'public' writing, I was nervous about the whole activity. However, all the students were most supportive and said that the exercise had given them a much clearer idea of what is meant by 'modelling' and 'thinking aloud'. They commented further that all too often college lecturers *talk* about teaching methods without giving practical demonstrations of how the methods may be implemented.

The National Curriculum suggests that at level 5 in the writing process, pupils should be able to: write in a variety of forms for a range of purposes and audiences in ways which attempt to engage the interest of the reader. Beard considers that there are four basic purposes for which people write. Firstly, there is writing of a personal nature, sometimes expressed for the writer only. It may be found in diaries, journals and written prayers. Secondly, there is writing which informs and in which emphasis will be on reproducing some aspect of the reality of that world in reports, brochures, recipes, labels, instructions and so on. Thirdly, there is writing to entertain which includes stories, poems, jokes and songs. Beard adds that this kind of writing will be more concerned with the language itself, getting the best words in the best order, and will normally follow some sort of literary convention or poetic tradition. Fourthly, there is persuasive writing in which the emphasis is on the audience and the possibility of changing behaviour or attitude. Such writing is seen in advertising, debate and argument where 'proof' or 'logic' are used more subjectively and where emotional appeals and shrewdly planned rhetorical techniques are often involved. Drawing upon the communication triangle model of James Kinneavy (1971), Beard guesses though that 'compared with the reading of fiction, normally presented in a predominantly narrative mode, children have very little non-fiction read to them' (1984, p. 18). Similarly, Alison Littlefair (1989, p. 181), suggests that teachers should include strategies which involve even quite young pupils in hearing texts from different genres in order that they may subconsciously develop their awareness of textual patterns. Later, pupils may be helped to compare and discuss books of different genres. In fact, Hall (1992) refers to a teacher of reception children who established a hotel in the play area. Before children could play there, they had to apply for a job in the hotel.

> The class discussed what jobs would be available and talked about what an application might involve. The children then wrote their applications. At the age of five they were independently creating assertive texts. (p. 3)

As Littlefair points out though, such instruction is only possible if teachers themselves have an understanding of language patterning and thus can balance genres of reading material. There are important possibilities here for initial teacher training to do much more to prepare student teachers to become *effective* teachers of reading and writing; an awareness of different genres seems essential if children are to write for different purposes, audiences and in different modes. All these recommendations highlight the fact that teachers need to plan lessons and time extremely carefully if they are to 'expose' children to a wide range of fiction, popular and classic and non-fiction of varying genres.

Though concentrating mainly on the writing process as a *whole*, Beard makes some relevant observations regarding spelling instruction. For example, he refers to the fact that most published spelling lists;

> . . . do not build in the necessity to carry out some kind of
> exploration to establish whether or not children can
> already spell the lists they provide for teaching. Teachers
> who methodically introduce five words a day to children
> and test the week's twenty on Friday can easily overlook this
> paradox, while also neglecting to help children develop a
> strategy for learning the words they need. (1984, p. 127)

This observation is supported by his reference to reports by Her Majesty's Inspectorate (HMI) (DES, 1978, 1982) which indicated that the teaching of spelling seemed to be systematically undertaken in some schools and neglected in others. Moreover, in schools where attention was given to spelling, it seemed that word lists, dictation, copying, correcting errors and learning lists of words for homework predominated. (These strategies will be discussed further in the chapters on teaching spelling.)

Like Peters and Todd, Beard considers that children's spelling should be based on pupils' needs according to their writing, and that teachers should develop an interest in letter patterns within their children. Also, like Peters, he recommends the Look/Cover – Write/Check method of learning spellings, and the entry of words which have been causing difficulty into children's personal dictionaries. Additionally, Beard recommends that teachers too have personal dictionaries 'to note down common uncertainties within a class and other points of interest' (1984, p. 125). This is, in my opinion, vital since it is all too easy for busy teachers to forget what has been causing difficulties only one or more days earlier.

Summary

Hall, Robinson and Czerniewska have shown that children's earliest writings reflect their experiences of literacy (at home and school), and these writings also evidence their knowledge of the writing process, albeit in a form in which 'rules' have been invented by them. In these earliest stages, teachers are urged to accept children's unaided writings for what they are, and what they mean to the child while, at the same time, using them to note the child's development (or difficulties) in the writing process. As children are seen to have gained knowledge about the writing process and traditional orthography, teachers should lead them to an awareness of likely combinations of letter strings and help the children to develop an interest in words and language.

As children grow older and (presumably) develop as writers, Graves and Beard in particular are concerned that teachers should not react to children's work by simply inspecting for flaws (especially spelling flaws). Both emphasise that teachers should involve child writers in positive discussion about the work done, and play an active part in helping children to plan, compose and review work; this includes allowing children to observe them planning written work while 'thinking aloud' as they work on OHPs or large sheets of paper. Beard stresses, too, the wider range of purposes and audiences for which children may write, and the need to provide them with experiences of listening to and discussing non-fiction. Graves and Beard consider that children must be exposed to a wide range of literature and poetry in order to promote children's love of language and the development of their vocabulary and written work. Both regard spelling as an *integral* part of the writing process; Beard (like Peters) states that in order to improve spelling, many children will need the systematically planned experiences of school to help them to 'look at words in special ways' (1984, p. 120).

The overall message is then, that spelling should be embedded in writing, reading and language processes and not merely a study of letters and words in isolation, unrelated to class work or children's needs. As Carty (1992) said, 'We must always remember that the goal of spelling instruction should be to develop the ability of children to communicate their thoughts and ideas to others. It must not, therefore, be seen as an end in itself' (p. 22).

Earlier in this chapter, reference was made to Peters' view of the developmental stages through which children pass in their spelling. Thus, the next chapter will concern itself with how teachers may assess spelling progress, promote spelling progress, and detect difficulties within the context of children's writing.

5 Spelling assessment (within the writing process)

I must point out that this chapter is not concerned with assessment based on weekly spelling tests of lists of words, for as Gerald Carty (1992) stated about his two children, one of whom was a weak speller, the other being an excellent speller, 'Both achieved 100% success on almost all of the weekly Friday spelling tests' (p. 17), thus emphasising the misleading results we may obtain if we judge spelling progress in isolation from written work. This chapter *is* concerned mainly with assessing what counts as progress within the writing process, and also assessing what may be causing specific difficulties in spelling as evidenced by children's writing. Similarly, the National Curriculum for teaching English includes teachers' considerations of children's vocabulary, spelling, handwriting and punctuation under the heading of 'Writing'. However, David Pascall on behalf of the National Curriculum Council (1992), advised the Secretary of State that the present separation of spelling (AT4) and handwriting (AT5) from writing (AT3) implies that the mechanisms of writing are in some way separate from the whole process of written communication. They recommend, therefore, that ATs4, 5 and 4/5 be amalgamated into one attainment target, AT3, entitled 'Writing including spelling, grammar and handwriting'.

The National Curriculum states further: 'Teachers will want to adopt approaches to the gathering of evidence about their pupils' attainments which suit their own teaching style' (1990, E1, 1.1) and 'Involving children in self-assessment helps them to a better understanding of their own strengths and needs' (1990, E1, 1.4.)

Indeed, the findings of a survey carried out by Vivienne Cato *et al.* (1992) for the National Federation of Educational Research (NFER) indicated that, despite the National Curriculum's introduction of Standard Assessment Tasks, many teachers preferred to make their own informal assessments of progress in reading and writing. The main aim of the survey was to investigate the range of methods and approaches used by teachers in year 2 in teaching reading and writing (p. 2). However, the researchers observed that much of the information gathered about reading and writing through informal methods was not effectively conveyed to others involved in the children's education which, in some cases, included the child concerned. The researchers stated:

> In the main, teachers appeared to have little time to devote
> to the close scrutiny and discussion of children's work. (p. 36)

Another significant finding was that many teachers were aware of their own lack of expertise in identifying and teaching children with incipient reading difficulties (p. 38). Since the researchers referred to writing as the 'poor cousin' (when compared with reading), it may be concluded that the preceding observations could also be applied to children with incipient writing difficulties.

The researchers found too a lack of consensus in teachers' assumptions about their pupils' levels of performance. In fact, their analysis of pupils' writing revealed a range of achievement:

> . . . from work which would be warmly received in the
> nursery to some which would not be out of place in the
> upper years of primary school. (p. 36)

Cato *et al.* suggested that a starting point from which teachers could reach consensus of opinion would be their review of exemplary scripts which reflect the range of performance among pupils concerned (p. 37).

It seems then, that assessment is a subject which seems to cause difficulties for some teachers. Often it appears that we teachers are more at ease with putting some very general comments on work, such as 'Well done, Peter!' or 'A very good story, Anne' or 'Your work is untidy and your spelling is poor.' Clearly, such remarks are unhelpful in terms of marking progress or for helping the child to overcome difficulties. Yet, if teachers are to help themselves as well as the children (and possibly parents) to be aware of progress and problems (supplying special support for the latter), it is essential that they acquaint themselves with methods whereby children's work may be assessed critically and constructively. It is, therefore, intended to consider firstly how teachers (and parents) may assess the development of young writers from the age of 3 years to the age of 6 years, and also promote further progress based on what they write. (As we saw in Chapter 4, children's earliest scribbles represent their first attempts at the writing process.) Secondly, it is intended to describe ideas put forward by a teacher for screening and assessing children's writing behaviour after four terms at school. Thirdly, methods of categorising spelling development and difficulties via analyses of spelling errors will be discussed.

The development of invented spelling in young writers

In level 1 of the spelling attainment target in the National Curriculum, it is stated that pupils should be able to:

a) Begin to show an understanding of the difference between drawing and writing, and between numbers and letters.

b) Write some letter shapes in response to speech sounds and letter names.

c) Use at least single letters or groups of letters to represent whole words or parts of words.

Level 2 of the spelling attainment target states that pupils should be able to:

a) Produce recognisable (though not necessarily always correct) spelling of a range of common words.

b) Spell correctly, in the course of their own writing, simple monosyllabic words they use regularly which observe common patterns.

c) Recognise that spelling has patterns and begin to apply their knowledge of those patterns in their attempts to spell a wider range of words.

d) Show knowledge of the names and order of the letters of the alphabet.

In the following examples of children's work, we shall consider the child's level of development, and suggestions will be made regarding the instruction parents and teachers *may* give to enable the child to make progress in his or her writing and spelling.

It has been observed that the very first marks of progress in the young child is evidenced when he or she shows the marks on paper to be meaningful by explaining what they represent (see 3-year-old Shaun's representation of a church, figure 5.1).

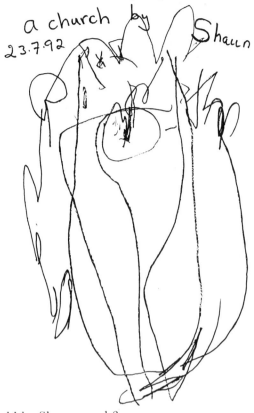

Figure 5.1 'A church' by Shaun, aged 3 years

At this stage, it is probably sufficient for adults to ask open-ended questions, such as 'Which church is this?' and 'Can you tell me more about the church?' By this means, Shaun may be involved in a meaningful discussion which places importance on his drawing. Following this stage come drawings which are recognisable (see figure 5.2 which shows 4-year-old Steven's picture of a spider).

Steven should be praised for his lively picture of a spider. Again, it is suggested that the drawing is discussed via questions, such as 'Where have you seen spiders?', 'How many legs has your spider?' and 'Do you know any rhymes about spiders?' It seems a good idea to write the word 'Spider' on the picture as Steven watches. Perhaps his attention could be drawn to the formation of the letter 'S' and its sound. The letter 'S' could also be related to the 'S' in his name.

Drawings which reflect yet a further stage are accompanied by 'writing' (see figure 5.3). Though this 5 year old's own writing does not show clearly defined letters in traditional orthography, the child is indicating an

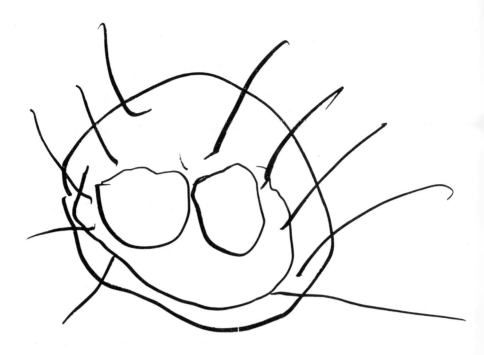

Figure 5.2   At a later stage, children produce drawings which others may recognise

understanding of the difference between drawing and writing (National Curriculum, level 1).

After some discussion about the scene on the beach, this child could be introduced to two words which connect speech sounds to writing. I suggest that 'I am' is well within her capabilities since she is already forming shapes which resemble 'a' and 'm'. It is important that the child observes the letters being formed correctly by the adult.

In figure 5.4, we see that Jenny (aged 5 years) is able to write her own name and her letters have become more defined, though they are randomly interspersed with numbers as she writes about the obstacle race on sports' day. (See 1a, National Curriculum.)

Jenny's picture is worthy of praise and discussion. Her name is clearly identifiable, though her formation of 'j', 'n' and 'y' need attention. I am not sure if it is better to concentrate firstly on the 'j' and 'y' (whose tails go to the right rather than the left), and secondly on the 'ns' (whose stalks

I am on the beach

Figure 5.3   A further stage of development reveals children producing drawings accompanied by 'writing'

are placed on the right rather than the left), or whether to discuss the formation of all three letters at one session. All depends on the individual child and his or her potential learning 'load'.

When children begin to use the first letters of words which they wish to write, they are showing tremendous progress in terms of understanding how the English spelling system works. In figure 5.5 on page 73 we see that Stephen (aged 5 years) illustrates also that he knows about the left to right sequence of our writing system. He has included, too, a word he has learned in its traditional form (is), and he illustrates his ability to copy (almost correctly) from a label on the classroom wall (shops). (See 1c, National Curriculum.)

I think Stephen is ready to learn the spelling of the common (but irregular) word 'my'. His attention could also be drawn to the label 'shops' in the classroom, and he could be asked to spot the letter missing from his spelling. Perhaps this could be his introduction to the Look/Cover – Write/Check method of spelling.

Emma (figure 5.6 on page 74) illustrates her understanding of the concept of a word as a separate unit; her words (made up of the first and last sounds of the words she wishes to write) show also the influence of 'Get well' cards which sometimes have only two or three words per line. (See 1c, National Curriculum.)

Jenny aged 5 - sports day - the obstacle race.

Figure 5.4 'Writing' by Jenny, aged 5 years

Since 'get' and 'well' required the vowel 'e' (sounded in its short form), it seems a good idea for the teacher to articulate the short 'e' sound while forming it visually. The teacher could then write out the words 'get' and 'well', saying the words as they are written. Emma could try to write the words from memory. Other words with these 'patterns' could also be discussed, for example: let, met, pet, set, bell, fell, sell, tell.

Development from this stage is the increasing use of traditional spellings along with invented spelling (see 5-year-old Cathy's work, figure 5.7). Though the words in the third line of her work merge together, the space between words is quite well defined in the second line of writing. Her invented spellings of night (nath), played (blayd) and bike (pice) show an interesting 'cross-fertilisation' between what she hears and the visual aspects of the words. There is some confusion of the letters p/b; however, b-d-p-q are frequently confused by learners in the early stages of reading and writing since they are all characterised by 'a circle and a stick'. Also, Temple *et al.* (1988) (see Chapter 3) suggested that certain sounds are made in similar ways and so it could be that Cathy is not able to differentiate

Figure 5.5 When children begin to use the first letters of the words they wish to write, they have made great progress

clearly between the sound of 'b' and 'p'. Cathy seems to be recalling the 'ht' at the end of 'night' as she writes 'nath', moreover, her final 'e' on the end of 'pike' suggests good visual recall. Words spelled correctly are: I - have - got - a - ball - it - is - last - on - my. (See 2a,b,c, National Curriculum.)

I suggest that, after giving credit to Cathy for the content *and* presentation of her writing, the teacher discusses explicitly with Cathy how we form and sound 'p'. This could be followed by a study of words (oral and visual) beginning with 'p' (including ('play') with Cathy going on to suggest more words which she *thinks* begin with 'p'. Depending on how well Cathy responds to this instruction, the formation and sound of the letter 'b' may then be discussed and followed by a similar oral/visual study of words beginning with 'b' (suggested, if possible, by Cathy). Note that the child is not being taught how to spell the p/b words, but merely to differentiate the sounds and formation in this *one* period of instruction.

Note too that there is a great diversity in levels of ability in children who are aged 5 years, even in the small sample of children shown here.

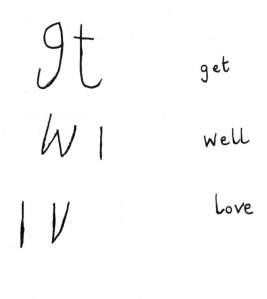

get

well

Love

Figure 5.6 Emma understands the concept of a word as a separate unit

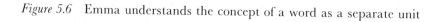

Figure 5.7 Children's use of a mixture of traditional and invented spelling marks positive progress

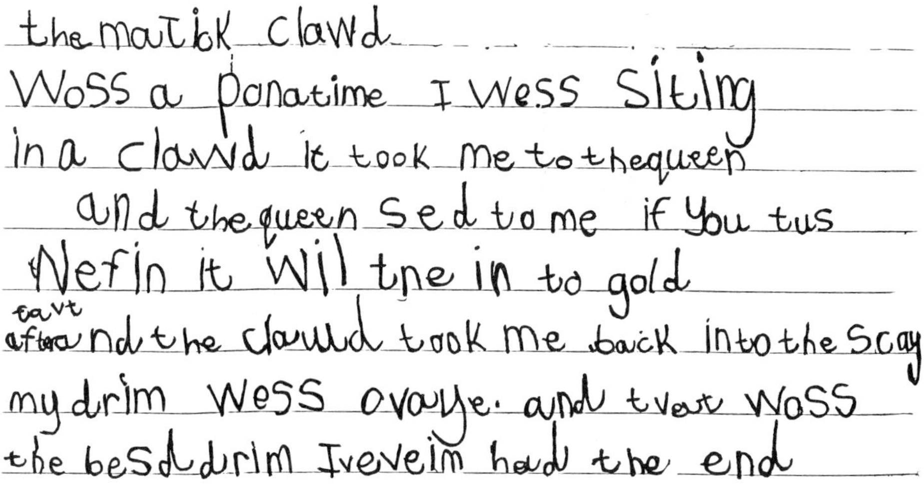

the mațok clawd
Woss a ponatime I wess Siting
in a clawd it took me to thequeen
and the queen sed to me if you tus
Nefin it Wil tne in to gold
aftoav nd the clawd took me back into the Scay
my drim wess ovaye. and tvat woss
the besd drim Iveveim had the end

Figure 5.8 Narrative writing by Leigh, aged 6 years, illustrating his phonological usage of language

The piece of narrative writing by Leigh, aged 6 years (figure 5.8) is very interesting.

> The Magic Cloud
> Once upon a time I was sitting in a cloud it took me to the
> queen and the queen said to me if you touch anything it
> will turn into gold after that and the cloud took me back into
> the sky my dream was over and that was the best dream
> I've ever (im?) had the end.

Leigh's writing reflects his integration of a known story (King Midas) into his own work and also his extensive use of the phonological aspects of our language in his writing. It also illustrates Leigh's interpretation of the word-division at the beginning of traditional stories and his (possible) *lack* of awareness of the end 'ch' sound in 'touch' (tus). His invented spelling is very logical and highlights what Goswami and Bryant (1990) say about children's invented spellings in general and, in particular, their comments regarding children's use of alphabet names as well as sounds in their writing, for example, Nefin (anything). Similarly scay (sky) reflects Leigh's acute phonological awareness of the sounds within the word. (Goswami and Bryant (1990) were referred to in Chapter 3.)

After praising Leigh for writing so vividly about his dream, I think it advisable to consider aurally and visually the word 'was', spelled three times as 'WOSS', and the word 'once', also spelled as 'WOSS'. Though Leigh spells some words correctly, he is generally over-dependent on phonological knowledge, which means that certain sounds are obscured, such as the 'n' in 'once'. Perhaps the teacher could write, for example, the sentence '*Once* I *was* sitting in a cloud.' The sentence could then be read to the child with 'was' and 'once', in particular, being articulated very clearly by the teacher and the words being pointed to simultaneously. Teacher and child could read the sentence together several times. Leigh could then learn: was, one/once (and *perhaps* sitting and cloud) and write them in a sentence.

Six-year-old Andrew's narrative (Fig. 5.9) reflects imagination, the ability to sequence events and very logical invented spellings based on what he hears. Note that the replacement of 'th' by 'f' is quite common in young children's speech and commented on by Temple *et al.* (1988) in Chapter 3. (We saw this, too, in Leigh's work – Nefin.) Though there is no use of punctuation, Andrew's work is not dominated by 'ands'. He is showing some awareness of the 'ck' blend in our language (brock), and like the child in Figure 10, he evidences recall of quite a high proportion of traditional spellings: the - green - were - for - went - into - shop - and - with - it. (See 2a,b,c, National Curriculum.)

Andrew should be praised for his imaginative story and perhaps asked to recall what 'things' the astronauts were looking for. It is possibly time to draw his attention to the 'th' digraph in our language; the idea that two letters can make one sound is often a difficult concept for novice writers (as Temple *et al.* (1980) stated, see Chapter 3). The teacher could write and articulate the words 'thing' and 'they' explaining how the 'th' is formed (noting that 'th' is formed slightly differently in the two words). Words studied might include: thing, thin, they, this, that. Andrew might then learn a sentence, such as 'I think they are thin things.'

Figure 5.10 shows Amy's record (explanation) of practical work carried out in a science lesson. She was aged 6 years, 7 months. It is quite a sophisticated piece of work since putting in sequence the making of a truck is by no means an easy task. In fact, it is not until level 4 of attainment targets for writing in the National Curriculum that children are expected to write 'accounts or explanations, perhaps of a scientific investigation'. Also, Amy's work shows an awareness of full stops, so clearly she is on the way to some understanding in this area. Like Andrew, she substitutes 'f' for 'th' in her writing (thought/fort, through/frow). She also substitutes 'v' for 'th' in 'an nuvare' (another). Unlike Andrew, but like most children of her age, she is using the conjunction 'and' to link her statements. The number

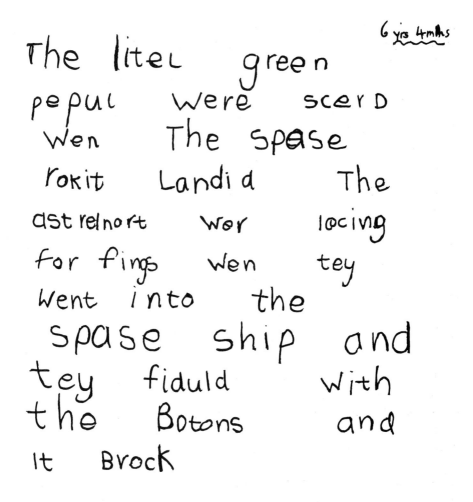

6 yrs 4mths

The litel green pepul were scerd Wen The spase rokit Landid The astrelnort wor locing for fings wen tey went into the spase ship and tey fiduld with the Botons and It Brock

Figure 5.9 6-year-old Andrew's narrative reveals very logical invented spelling and traditional spelling

of recalled traditional spellings is high: one - day - we - made - a - truck - of - in - some - wood - and - put - stuck - then - was - tested. Moreover, the work shows Amy's knowedge of the past tense, and though she ends 'finished' with a 't', tested and 'worked' (wrerced) have the common 'ed' ending.

Naturally, Amy should be praised for her ability to describe the making of a truck so well. In my opinion, two aspects of her writing need attention

Oct 12th 1990

One day We made a truck. We fort
of puting a howl. In Some wood and
We put some nels in the Wood and some
Weles. We stuck it to a pese of plastc
and we. Stuck an nuvare pese on and. We
put some stros. And put it frow an howl
then it was finisht and We tested it and
it wrerced.

(6yrs 7m)

Figure 5.10 This young child's work (copied out by her mother) reveals quite
sophisticated sequencing of events

in order to promote her progress, that is, her use of full-stops and her lack
of awareness of the digraph 'th'. Thus, I would firstly ask Amy to read
her text back to me and to make a long pause (or stop) whenever she
used a full-stop. I hope that she would realise that her full-stops were
sometimes preventing her text from making sense. Then I would write in
my suggestions for the placing of full-stops (as recommended by Donald
Graves, see Chapter 4) and ask Amy to read it back to me to note if my
full-stops helped her text to make sense. Secondly, I would draw Amy's
attention (aurally and visually) to the 'th' sound in *thought, through* and
another. Amy could choose how many of the three words she wanted to
learn. My suggestion would be thought/through (noting the '*ough*' letter
string) in a sentence, such as 'I thought it went through a hole.'

Clearly, the few examples shown here indicate children's tremendous
progress in the writing process from their earliest scribbles. It should
be stressed though that the teaching methods outlined were no more than
suggestions for responses to the children's work. Teachers (and parents) may
consider that other aspects of the children's writing needed more
immediate attention – and that is as it should be! I merely want to raise

adults' awareness of possible 'interactions' with children's work whereby the children's progress in writing is promoted, and sometimes it is sufficient to accept and talk positively about a child's work, omitting suggestions for improvement. Groups of teachers (and potential teachers) may learn much from each other if they make time to assess and comment upon a wide variety of children's writing at different levels of development (as recommended by Cato *et al.*, 1992). I was not the teacher of any of the children whose work has been discussed and so my 'interactions' were very generalised. For most texts, I would try to: give some praise to the child; encourage the child to talk about the content of his or her work; promote some progress in the writing process by means of brief instruction which would, ideally, be revised the next day. It would thus be vital that I made informal (but dated) notes regarding each child's progress/difficulties.

Screening tests in early years

Though we have seen that young children may make very positive progress in the writing process during their first year at school, it is by no means certain that all children will make the progress indicated by the examples given. Indeed, I often note that studies illustrating young children's work in, for example, writing, reading and language, seldom refer to the children who have difficulties in these areas. Sybil Hannovy (1991), however, asked the question:

> Why do reading and writing problems so often surface when children reach years 2 and 3? Is something happening [or not happening] in reception and year 1 that leads to this disaffection with reading and writing?. (p. 10)
> (The observation in parenthesis is mine.)

She concludes that teachers often wait too long before looking carefully at children's reading and writing behaviour for signs of confusion, and that two main areas which require investigation are: attitudes to literacy and perceptual difficulties. While working at the Cambridge Institute of Education, she constructed a screening test for year 1 to be given after children had been at school for four complete terms. Advantages of this test are that it can be given to up to 20 children at once by one teacher with another teacher in attendance and takes from 45 minutes to one hour to administer. (Since spelling is of paramount interest in this book, I have included only items which relate to that subject, thus Test 1, which deals with children's responses to descriptions and short stories, is omitted.)

To avoid copying, Hannovy suggests that children have 'screens' of folded card between them; the children may be told that the screens are to prevent other children from seeing how they do their puzzles and games. Also, there should be no writing or alphabets visible in the room.

Test 2, letter sounds

The teacher says words and repeats the initial sound. Children write the initial letter from memory. The two teachers have time to walk round and notice children's grip and posture, and also how they are forming their letters. If children cannot remember how to write a letter they put a dash. (I recommend that teachers make quite sure that children know what a dash is.)

Twenty or more letters may be given. Capitals may be marked as correct, but it should be noted where they are being used excessively.

Test 3a, written vocabulary

The children write all the words they can remember from memory in 5 minutes. Hannovy states that after four school terms most children can write at least six words from memory. (Marie Clay (1975) also recommends letting young children write words they know to determine the extent of their spelling vocabulary. Like Hannovy, Clay believes that children may be 'recovered' from potential failure in literacy by helping them to overcome any learning difficulties near the *beginning* of their schooling. See her *Reading Recovery* programme, 1990.)

Test 3b, three phonemes (units of significant sound)

Ten words are dictated, for example, rub, bit, men, and the children write those sounds they can hear. They put dashes if they cannot write a letter (I think the results of this test need careful consideration since, for example, children may be able to *hear* a phoneme, but not able to connect its sound with its visual representation). A mark is given for each sound correctly noted (even if the letter is reversed). For example, rub = Яod (scores 2, and the teacher notes the reversals and the substituted vowel sound); van = fa (scores 1, and the substitution of v/f is noted). After four terms, most children score 20 or more.

It is relevant to note that Suzanne Cataldo and Nick Ellis (1990) investigated the pattern of children's spelling development from the beginning of year 1 to year 2, and classified their spelling in five categories; these reflected an increasing insight into the phonetic structure of words (p. 115). Thus if the word to be spelled is 'cat', we might find it represented in one of the following ways:

1   c--, first letter only;
2   c-t, both 'boundaries' correct;
3   ca-, partially correct in sequence;
4   cet, only the middle phoneme is incorrect; and as Temple *et al.* (1988) pointed out, in construction, vowels are not very different from each other (p. 69);
5   cat, totally correct.

Test 3c, sentence dictation

The teacher dictates two sentences and repeats them several times slowly. The children attempt to write them using sounds and/or known whole words. A mark is given for each phoneme correctly identified (for example, sh-o-p would score 3 marks). Hannovy did not give any examples of sentences, but I presume that the sentences contain words familiar to the children (both orally and visually), and would include regular word patterns (in terms of sound/symbol correspondence) and also irregular word patterns in familiar words (for example, go, the, to). Though this test is not a standardised test, it has been used in 14 schools; it seems then that it is a useful model from which teachers may construct their own screening tests for middle infants. It should be noted that the tests highlight the child's ability (or lack of it) to connect phonemes with printed words, thus stressing the auditory aspect of our spelling system, rather than, as Peters (1985) suggests, the visual aspects. However, in the early stages of spelling, it seems essential that children make connections between what they hear and what they write in order to gain 'access' to our spelling system. This knowledge should be complemented by the visual memorisation of familiar, yet irregular words used by the children. (Though, as has been stated previously, the auditory/visual aspects of spelling will be discussed further in the chapters on teaching spelling.) I do think that teachers' consideration and construction of screening tests helps them to be aware of possible 'weak' links in their own teaching methods and, like Hannovy (1991) and Clay (1981), I consider the early detection of possible difficulties in the reading and writing processes is vital.

Categorisation of spelling difficulties via analyses of spelling miscues

In this chapter, we have seen that very young children are capable of using writing as a means of communication. It is important that in these early stages, teachers should, as Peters says (1975) 'accept and welcome' what young children write irrespective of how it is spelled (p. 6) otherwise they may see themselves not as writers with something to say, but as poor spellers. (This means that testing like that described by Hannovy (1991) should be treated, as she suggests, like a game. Moreover, I feel strongly that the results should *never* be communicated to the children; they are purely a means of detecting children with potential difficulties in the writing process. Indeed, teachers may prefer to devise some means of assessing young children's writing skills which is more informal than the method described by Hannovy). Of course, young children who ask teachers how to spell words or are able to use other spelling resources (which will be discussed in the chapters on teaching spelling) should be given every encouragement to do so. The transition from using mainly invented spellings to using traditional orthography should, for most children, be occurring before the end of year 1. However, as children progress in the variety and quality of their writing tasks, individual difficulties in spelling will, for some children, become more marked and, in these cases, children often need specific help. Testing which simply means marking a word correct or incorrect is of little value in terms of helping the child to overcome any difficulties. Just as Ken Goodman (1973) analysed children's oral reading errors (which he preferred to call miscues) in order to obtain information about reading strategies and to supply appropriate remediation if necessary, so several researchers have analysed children's spelling errors (which may similarly be termed spelling *miscues*) occurring in connected text in order to learn more about their spelling strategies. In the light of what the teacher finds out, children evidencing difficulties may be helped to use more appropriate spelling strategies.

Peters (1975) suggests that there are various categories of spelling miscues, and though she refers to five in total, it is intended to consider here only the four which, in her opinion, are 'the most revealing' (p. 22).

TABLE 1 Amended version of Peters' (1975) diagnostic and remedial spelling record sheet

WORD TO BE WRITTEN	1a REASONABLE PHONIC ALTERNATIVES (LETTER STRINGS)	1b PHONIC ALTERNATIVES NOT CON- FORMING TO SPELLING PRECEDENT	II FAULTY AUDITORY PERCEPTION	III PERSEVERATION	IV UNCLASSI- FIABLE MISCUES
certainly	ser, sir, cir	saer	suddenly thirteenly	cererertainly	
tied	tide, tighed	tarhd			
house	howse	hus			ship
ground			groung		oney
dangerous		danjrus		dangororous	

NB There is a mixture of my examples and Peters' examples in the above chart.

Table 1 is my amended version of Peters' diagnostic and remedial spelling record sheet. Peters considers that if a child's substitutions are mainly in column 1a, then the child is on its way to learning our coding system, and the prognosis is good. If they are mainly in 1b, then the child needs to attend to word structure, to likenesses and differences between words, and to learn common letter sequences.

If substitutions tend to be in column II, Peters suggests that it is wise to check the child's hearing (and the teacher's articulation!). Children who tend to substitute several words which evidence perseveration, may be copying 'blindly' and not paying attention to the word structure. When the number of unclassifiable errors is high, then a structured remedial or early spelling programme is essential.

Similarly, Jennifer Hepburn (1991) from Tasmania has written about children's spelling miscues, and thinks that children's spelling difficulties do not all originate from the same cause and thus remediation will vary. Basically, the categories she suggests are similar to those of Peters, though she names ten categories (including sub-divisions of main categories). For example, children whose spelling errors are usually reasonable phonic alternatives of the correct spelling (believe/beleave) have their errors categorised as 'Generalisations'. Just as Goodman (1973) considers some reading errors to be 'better' errors (for example, substituting 'home' for 'house'), so we can consider spelling errors which indicate that the novice writer is making generalisations as more positive errors; it is likely that the writer may need only minimal spelling instruction. Both Peters and Hepburn suggest that instruction may include looking carefully at other words with the same spelling pattern, and using cueing systems to help the child to remember the word. I think that a useful cueing sentence for the child writing 'beleave' might be 'I bel*ie*ve that the th*ie*f is not your fr*ie*nd.'

Moreover, I think that underlining the 'ie' pattern is essential in helping to reinforce the pattern in the child's memory process. Similarly, Peters suggests that the child who spells 'suit' as 'soot' may be given the sentence: 'The peng*ui*n spilt the fr*ui*t j*ui*ce down his black s*ui*t and r*ui*ned it.'

Children whose spelling miscues do not conform to spelling precedent (question/qeshun) are probably paying attention only to how words sound, and not how they look; thus there needs to be considerable time spent on words with similar spelling patterns which will help the child to become aware of possible letter sequences (for example, quest, question, queen, quit, mention, station, relation, nation).

Interestingly, Peters always stresses the visual aspect of words when teaching children with (or without) spelling difficulties, whereas Hepburn (p. 35) when discussing spellings which show reversals (house/huose; once/onec) states that part of remediation may include: 'Building word families with that sound' and 'Using sounding to test if the word could be right.' When considering children whose spelling miscues evidence incorrectly articulated words, Hepburn suggests that the child be shown the correct word in print and told how the word is articulated. Further remediation includes talking to the child and using any misarticulated words. Like Peters, Hepburn does not consider homophones (words with the same sound but a different meaning) as spelling errors, but rather as the wrong usage of the homophone (for example, 'to' written for 'too'). Children who confuse homophones need to be given a strategy for working out the correct homophone. She suggests that children confusing the preceding homophones be told 'Too means "a lot" and so it needs a lot of "oos"' (this seems to be a useful mnemonic, but children do at some point need to be aware that 'too' also means 'as well').

Hepburn makes no specific reference to words spelled in a seemingly bizarre manner (unclassifiable according to Peters). Peters suggests that such children who apparently have no spelling strategies should be taken back to the earliest stages of spelling studies, beginning with the child's name and address. Although I have found this strategy useful for novice spellers, I am not so sure that it is helpful for the novice speller who has apparently failed to develop a spelling system, since names and addresses are generally irregular in terms of sound/symbol correspondences. I think that they need to go through the stage of invented spelling where symbols may correspond to the sounds *they* hear and this includes making sure that they have knowledge about letter names and sounds. After this stage has been 'mastered', they should be then ready to move on to developing an awareness of the visual aspects of print and to exploring (and enjoying) the spelling patterns within their own name and address. (Children who are virtually non-spellers will be discussed in the chapter on children with spelling difficulties.)

Peters and Hepburn stress that children who have spelling difficulties should have their errors considered in connected text so that spelling strategies may be more easily noted in the context of writing. Of course, one must acknowledge that such analyses of children's spelling errors are time consuming when first undertaken but, as with learning any new skill, with its use comes both speed and perception. It seems clear that teachers, and especially student teachers, will benefit from group practice and instruction in the analyses of children's spelling miscues so that they may be alerted to patterns in spelling errors, and may thus speedily detect children with serious spelling difficulties.

Group discussions of spelling miscues and their possible causes may lead to dissension among the group, but it is such dissension/debate that generally promotes greater understanding of the subject under discussion. Moreover, assessment by means of miscue analysis need only be carried out two or three times a year, and only then with children who are experiencing spelling difficulties. As part of *ongoing* and informal assessment, Peters (1985, p. 101) recommends what she calls a 'Positive Assessment' of children's spelling strategies by which children are tested on misspellings in their own writing by means of dictated passages based on their writing. Peters considers that children's self-testing (and testing of each other) is vital as it promotes their responsibility for their own learning (a point stressed by Hepburn). However, Peters (1975) has also produced some dictated passages which may be used for diagnostic purposes to help children with spelling difficulties since, as she states:

> Unless what children write is controlled, the output is liable
> to show too much sample variability in quantity and subject.
> For this reason, diagnostic dictations related to children's
> word counts have been produced. These are 100 words
> in length and combine examples of the commonest types of
> deviant spelling. (1975, p. 17)

Peters' dictations are in the form of short stories which could well have been told by children of the relevant age range. For example, Peters' first dictation (for children aged 8–9 years) begins, 'One day, as I was walking down Bridge Street, I heard the sound of trotting.' Like Peters, I have constructed short dictation passages relevant to adults with spelling difficulties, based on their most common spelling errors. (Children's self-testing and the use of dictated sentences based on their difficulties will be discussed in the chapters on teaching spelling.)

Despite having produced dictated passages to help teachers to diagnose misspellings, Peters (1985) herself states that normative tests can never replace what good teachers know about individual difficulties. Moreover, I would suggest that good teachers are more likely to 'flourish' in schools where there is a 'whole-school' approach to the teaching of spelling. It surely must be helpful to the children if teachers in subsequent classes are continuing the same philosophy as their previous teachers. Conversely, confusion may occur (especially with respect to children with spelling difficulties) if subsequent teacher approach and emphasis is in opposition to what they have already experienced. For example, if one teacher stresses sounding out words to be spelled (perhaps into syllables), and another requires children to pay attention only to the visual aspect of words to be spelled, while a third insists that children use dictionaries to spell words, and a fourth teacher encourages children who need a word to go to them for help, then those children who have not developed their own spelling strategies may become even more confused. A 'whole school' policy might integrate all these strategies in a systematic manner, with infant and junior teachers working together to ensure that children fully understand the different techniques and their appropriateness under different circumstances. Moreover, the National Curriculum suggests that discussing records with colleagues can help teachers to become unbiased recorders (1990, English, E2, 1:7). This corresponds with the comments of Cato *et al.* (1992) (see page 67).

All initial teacher training courses now have 60 hours of contact time on English and another 40 hours on related study; this would seem to indicate that potential teachers will understand more of the practice and theory of this vital subject than has been indicated hitherto. Hanne Lambley (1992, pp. 21–2) gathered information about the teaching of reading from a survey involving a total of 192 teachers (over 80 per cent having had ten or more years of classroom experience), this indicated that most felt dissatisfied with their initial teacher training course, particularly with respect to the teaching of reading. It is possible that this applied also to knowledge about the writing process (and not just the sub-skill of spelling). There is, however, the likelihood that all initial teacher training will become 80 per cent (or more) school-based, and so it would seem that future initial teacher training courses will be slanted increasingly towards the practical side of teaching.

Additionally, initial teacher training courses must now provide students with a short course relating to the structure of language (its exact nature has not yet been specified). This is encouraging since, as Peters points out repeatedly, teachers need to develop their own knowledge about our English spelling system and its background if they are to promote an interest in our language in children. Knowledge obtained on such courses could be consolidated by 'in-service' courses related to our language. In fact, Lambley stated that many teachers felt that the most valuable part of their understanding of the teaching process occurred during 'in-service' training.

Summary

It seems then that teachers (and ideally parents, too) may observe novice writers' progress in the writing process by paying attention to the details in children's early 'writing' and drawings. Hannovy's suggestions for screening middle infants (or even younger children) may be used as a base upon which teachers may plan and develop screening tests relevant to the writing process and which are appropriate to the children they teach. In this way, children's difficulties (and progress) may be assessed early in their school life, and well before they begin to feel any sense of failure. Parents, too, if they are willing, may be involved in, and consulted about, any necessary remedial strategies.

Teachers' knowledge about children's spelling errors via analyses of spelling miscues should help them to approach children's writing in a positive manner, attending first to the content, yet also being aware of possible causes of any continued misspellings, and thus being able to help children to remedy any difficulties. As with any subject, the most effective teachers are the ones who have knowledge about their subject and who can thus inspire enthusiasm. Indeed, such teachers would be an invaluable source of practical knowledge if they were to be invited to share their expertise in teaching, assessment, record-keeping (and so on) with student teachers. They would also be an excellent source from which to obtain a wide variety of children's written work for students' discussion and assessment.

Important, too, is the sharing of ideas and knowledge about the writing process and its sub-skills by teachers in the same school. Thus, there may be standardisation of approach and priorities as teachers help children to become effective writers. Moreover, a common approach to writing may, in turn, help children develop an interest in our language and be clearer about the writing process in its many forms and why being an effective writer is a desirable accomplishment, and not just something they do to please God and Mrs Adde! (see page 55).

6 *Handwriting and spelling*

We have seen that educationalists like Peters (1985) and Beard (1984) consider that the ability to translate thoughts into effective written form is enhanced if the 'author' is able to write easily, speedily and legibly. Moreover, Peters considers that swift, well-formed handwriting is highly related to success in spelling, and that instruction in joined handwriting should begin *well* before the child reaches the junior school. Thus, it seems relevant to consider some of the ideas put forward regarding why and how handwriting and spelling may be taught together from a very early age. Since Charles Cripps and Robin Cox do this in their book *Joining the ABC* (1990), it is intended to outline some of their main and salient observations. It is also intended to refer to Rosemary Sassoon's main ideas on teaching handwriting detailed in *Handwriting – the way to teach it* (1990). Though her ideas generally coincide with those of Cripps and Cox, they do differ with respect to the extent to which handwriting may help children with their spelling, and also the age at which children should begin to join handwriting. The two books may serve as a starting point from which head teachers and teachers can develop and/or amend their own views on this subject. This chapter, then, will include past methods of teaching handwriting, reasons for and against teaching joined handwriting in the reception class, a discussion of some of the possible practical difficulties of teaching joined writing to young children, and a brief consideration of some of Cripps' and Cox's recommendations for teaching handwriting in a way that complements children's progress in spelling.

I must point out that during the 16 years which I spent as a teacher in primary schools, I never taught in a school where joined writing was introduced at five years, but nevertheless, I feel that there is much common sense in Cripps' and Cox's book which is worthy of consideration, together with Sassoon's cautionary notes regarding spelling and handwriting. The authors refer firstly to the emphasis on free expression and creativity which became widespread during and after the Second World War. With the encouragement of more imaginative writing, and also with teaching an integrated day, correspondingly less emphasis was placed on the structured teaching of handwriting. Cripps and Cox also refer to the main methods by which handwriting was 'taught' in many schools: this often consisted of the young child watching the teacher writing down his or her 'talk' under the pictures drawn in his or her book. The teacher would then move away to the next child while he or she tried to imitate what the teacher had done. This often proved very difficult since much guesswork was involved, especially with respect to where to start copying the letter shapes. In fact, often no direct teaching was involved, and later inspection by the teacher, when the letters had been formed, did not reveal the difficulties or misunderstandings which the child may have experienced. However, a more formal approach to teaching handwriting is spreading, and the National Curriculum (1990) refers to legible handwriting at levels 1 and 2. Not until level 3, though, is it stated that pupils should be able to produce 'clear and legible joined-up writing' (Target 5: handwriting).

Cripps and Cox feel that the *means* by which legible handwriting is reached are largely ignored and, moreover, that joined writing should be taught on the child's entry into school. They acknowledge that most schools which commence joined writing in the junior department do so because reading schemes, books, cards, classroom notices, etc., are all in printed form and, thus, these schools consider that matters are simplified if children learn to write by copying the writing forms that they read. However, Cripps and Cox state, 'This may seem very straightforward and sensible but these schools are considering reading not spelling' (p. 21). They go on to put forward the case for teaching joined writing on entry into school and they refer firstly to the *disadvantages of print script* which include the following observations:

- Print script does not follow on from the free scribble movements that children make when they first hold a pencil.

- When children learn print script first, they have to make a 'break' to learn joined writing. Many children revert later to the disconnected letters that they first learned and this may impede speedy (and legible) note-taking.

- Often children do not learn how to space letters in print writing correctly. (In joined writing, the joining stroke makes a natural space between two letters.)

- With print script there is no flow from one letter to another. Concentration is on individual letters.

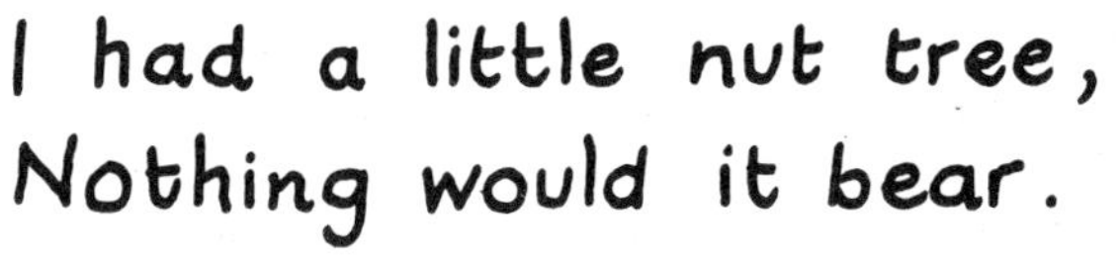

I had a little nut tree,
Nothing would it bear.

Figure 6.1   A typical example of print script

I had a little nut tree,
Nothing would it bear.

Figure 6.2   Marion Richardson's round handwriting style

Secondly, Cripps and Cox consider the *advantages of joined writing* about which they make the following observations:

- There is no 'break' in handwriting style in the junior department.

- From very early stages, children acquire the concept of a 'word' since joined letters form words which are separated from each other.

- Correct letter formation is ensured from the beginning (I feel that this should also apply to schools which teach printing on school entry). Spelling is helped since letter strings are necessarily connected when writing a word (though as we shall see, Sassoon challenges this viewpoint). The authors state that children must also 'be taught to make visual associations between words' (p. 24). I think explicit teaching is vital since not all children make connections between letter strings in different words unless the connections are explicitly pointed out. Implicitness in the language used by some teachers when giving instruction to children (and adults) may be a barrier to some children's (and adults') effective learning (see Mudd, 1987, 1990b).

They state, too:

> . . . one of the major reasons for teaching joined writing
> from the beginning is to enable children by the age of
> 7 years, just when the desire to write is reaching its fullest
> momentum, to have mastery over this particular skill.
> (p. 26)

However, Sassoon considers that the idea of continuous writing helping with spelling is open to question. In the first place, she does not think that all 5-year-old children have the co-ordination to perform more than a simple baseline join in their early writing. Thus, she suggests a printing style in which all letters that terminate on the baseline be given an exit stroke (for example, a, c, d, e, h, i). She states:

> With straight print script letters, maximum pressure is on the
> baseline, but with an exit the pencil pressure is relaxed as the
> upstroke changes direction and lifts towards the next letter.
> This is what promotes a relaxed flowing writing, whether
> joined or not. An exit stroke also builds in a space between
> letters. (p. 5)

Secondly, even when children are joining their writing (at about 7 years) Sassoon does not think that *continuous* joined writing is a good idea since:

> . . . the hand needs a chance to move along the line, so
> pen-lifts are not only permissible but essential during long
> words. (p. 13)

She continues:

> Poor spellers often find ten or twelve letter words easier to
> work out when they are broken up into smaller sections.

(The breaking up of words to be spelled into sections is a controversial area, and will be discussed in the chapter on teaching spelling.) However, she goes on to say:

> Common letter sequences, and common two or three letter
> words are useful practice when young children are
> learning to join. (p. 14)

Sassoon's ideas on baseline exit strokes seem to be a good preparation for children joining their writing, though I am not sure about her earlier observations regarding poor spellers who find 10 and 12 letter words easier to work out if they break them into smaller sections. In my experience, many poor spellers make breaks in long *or* short words because they sound out what they hear. The words are thus written 'bit by bit'. It would seem that a joined handwriting *plus* attention to the visual aspects of words would be helpful to poor spellers.

Later in their book, Cripps and Cox consider some of the practical difficulties which teachers may feel will arise if young children are introduced to joined writing. Major difficulties are put into the form of questions to which the authors respond. Some of the questions and answers are outlined below and I have generally indicated whether or not Sassoon supports their views.

Will children be able to read joined writing?

The authors feel that the idea of children finding joined writing difficult to read is probably based on tradition and misapprehension. In fact, in schools where joined writing is taught from the beginning, a common comment is 'I believe that we have been underestimating children all the time' (p. 20). In one school, the reception teacher who used *Breakthrough to Literacy Material* to teach reading, had in the third week of term a group of children who could read approximately 15 words. She presented these words on identical cards and in joined writing. The children were asked to match both sets of words and, without further explanation, were able to pick out the pairs. Cripps and Cox conclude that the only practical implications for teachers are that children should have the chance to read both print and joined writing. They suggest, too, that perhaps any teacher-produced material for reading should be in print, but that any displays should be written in the school's handwriting style. Sassoon similarly feels that children see letters of all kinds on television and in advertisements and soon learn to decipher different forms of various letters.

Breakthrough to Literacy (Mackay *et al.*, 1970) treats learning to read and write as part of the language development process. Basically, its apparatus provides children with a wide range of word cards which are relevant to children's language and may be added to. There are also plastic stands in which children can insert word cards to construct their own personal sentences. In this way, children:

> . . . are able to build up expectations of what words, phrases
> and sentences look like, and they are free to say what is
> important to them. (Teacher's Manual, 1981, p. 7)

The Teacher's Manual also contains a section on handwriting in which
they point out the dangers of urging children to express ideas in their
own handwriting before they have acquired the skills of correctly formed
writing and what they term as 'orderly' (as opposed to random) spelling.
They maintain that:

> . . . slow and clumsy handwriting and insecure spelling are
> likely to ensure that a child will view any writing task with
> dismay. (p. 103)

What kind of perceptual activities will help children to differentiate between letters and joins (ligatures)?

Jigsaws, looking at patterns, using matching materials, and spot-the-
difference games all help to increase children's visual activity. The
authors stress too the importance of a great deal of oral work relating to
the physical shaping of letters, as this helps children to 'see' the whole
letter. For example, in teaching the letter 'g', the teacher might say, 'Start
at the dot and come back round and up to the dot: now straight down
and curl round to make a swing for someone to sit in.' (The starting point
or 'dot' of the letter 'g' would be g Some teachers (see page 98) refer
to this starting point as 'one o'clock'. The authors go on to say that if the
separate letter is already well-established, the join often follows quite
naturally. In one school, referred to by Cripps and Cox, reception children
were asked to count or point to the letters and joins in a prepared piece of
writing. The children easily identified letters or joins.

Do 5 year olds have the motor control for joining letters?

While acknowledging that children should not be 'pushed' into forming
letters before their hand and eye co-ordination and their ability to perceive
or copy are sufficiently developed, Cripps and Cox maintain that young
children may undergo stages of what they call 'writing readiness', which
include being aware of patterns around them, making their own patterns

and finally seeing the relationship between letters and patterns. Consequently, they state that children should not be asked to record with a pencil and paper too early, that is, before letter formation has been firmly established. Similarly, Sassoon (1990) considers that children should not write 'news' etc. until all letters are correctly formed. It is worth noting that such statements are in direct contrast with the views of Nigel Hall (referred to in Chapter 4). He described literacy related work undertaken by reception and nursery children, many of whom were aged between 3 and 5 years. Hall *et al.* (1987) observe:

> Those children were not waiting for formal schooling to use their literacy but they were waiting for the opportunity to display their use of it. (p. 143)

Presumably, many of these children were 'writing' before they had been taught correct letter formation. Sassoon, however, tells of recent attitudes regarding young children by which teachers encourage them to 'play with letters and not correct or teach anything that might inhibit them from expressing their creativity'. She goes on to say that as soon as children can write the letters of their names, correct letter formation should be taught. She warns that if this is not done, 'incorrect movements become habits that are progressively difficult to alter' (1990, p. 2). And, as we have seen, Peters' research indicates that well-formed handwriting is highly related to success in spelling.

Naturally, Cripps and Cox realise that some children are 'writers' before they commence school, and they suggest that children who have learned to write before school entry should be encouraged to produce inventive writing in any way they wish. They suggest that teachers do not force children into the 'blind' copying of letters or words which have yet to be taught, and yet there may be problems caused by children who have acquired incorrect habits of letter formation which are often difficult to correct. In such instances, teachers may work in small groups with the children so that correct letter formation is gradually achieved.

Alternative methods of recording thoughts or experiences are suggested by Cripps and Cox. Among their suggestions are:

- *Breakthrough to literacy*. The children make their own sentences using either the teacher's or their own sentence stand. These sentences may be read to the teacher, and then recorded by the teacher in the child's book (using print or joined script).

- *Typists*. Children gain immense satisfaction from dictating a story to a person who is proficient on the keyboard. (I wonder if older children or parents may be useful here.)

- *Serial sketches*. Pictures drawn by the children in serial form may serve to recall an experience or to record a story. (From experience, I know that children do not always find this activity easy unless given adequate instruction.)

- *Tape recordings*. Children can soon become proficient at using a tape recorder (if given explicit instruction). By careful use of the pause button, a good story can be recorded for other people. (Again, I wonder if interested parents familiar with the school's policy on writing might be helpful in transposing the oral work to a written form.)

Will children be confused when copying from a printed form?

The authors' experience suggests that if the formation of letters is well taught then children should not have any particular difficulty in seeing a printed word and writing it in joined form (they give an example of a 5-year-old child's conversion of a printed poem to joined writing (p. 37)). They stress the importance of the teacher presenting a joined style when writing in children's books. Similarly, Sassoon stresses the importance of teachers using correctly formed writing in children's books and for display.

Will children who move either from or into a school that teaches joined writing suffer setbacks?

Cripps and Cox feel that teachers who are sensitive to any possible writing difficulties evidenced by children moving from a school with a different approach to teaching writing will generally help the children to avoid setbacks in their writing. Teachers should be prepared to spend time helping to diffuse any potential problems. Moreover, the authors maintain that the greatest problems are posed by children who have learned incorrect letter formation. Sassoon states: 'If there is a policy of ensuring the correct movement of letters then some kind of tactful assessment will be needed to see that a new pupil's letters have no important movement faults' (1990,

p. 21). It appears then that the case for teaching joined writing at an early age has been supported and accompanied by useful suggestions for overcoming any possible difficulties. However, even if teachers decide (either through choice, or the dictate of the school policy) that joined writing should begin in the junior department, it seems to me that many of Cripps' and Cox's and Sassoon's suggestions for teaching handwriting in general are both valid and helpful. As Peters (1970, p. 68) observed, children who have a swift control of handwriting write in groups of letters in connected form and this effects qualitative progress in their spelling behaviour. Thus, some of Cripps', Cox's and Sassoon's main recommendations for teachers of handwriting will be outlined briefly.

Whole school policies and involvement of parents and pre-school leaders

The authors remind head teachers to make sure that new members of staff receive a well-structured and meaningful induction programme regarding the teaching of writing. Moreover, schools in which joined writing is taught in reception classes should ensure that all the teachers understand the theory behind the principle of teaching joined writing to young children. In schools where there is a changeover of writing policy, the support of parents and pre-school leaders is central to success; thus there should be meetings to explain the rationale behind the change and also to give instructions in the best ways to help children with their writing. Parents may be invited to help with the group teaching of writing in the classroom, though they should, for obvious reasons, never be given continuous responsibility for a group. Naturally, teachers' own styles of writing within the classroom should reflect the style being taught to the children. Cripps, Cox and Sassoon all point out that in the *early* stages of either joined writing, or print which has baseline exit strokes, children's writing is often less neat in appearance than print. Neatness (and flow) generally come later as handwriting skills are improved. I think that all interested 'parties' should be made aware of this probability when discussing handwriting policies.

Classroom organisation for writing instruction

Generally, the authors recommend group sizes of six to ten children for reception and year 1 children and slightly larger groups for older children (with children grouped according to ability). Groups receiving chalk-and-talk instruction should face the blackboard. Among obvious advantages from the children's viewpoint is the fact that the teacher, watching children tracing in the air, can more easily identify incorrect movements. (Beard (1984, p. 66), also makes the point that if air-writing is used, it is clearly important for teachers' instruction to be given looking back at the children over the shoulder.)

Left-handed children

Left-handers should always sit to the left of a right-hander. This will avoid their arms colliding. The left-hander must have the paper to the left of the mid-line of the body and about 5 centimetres away with the light coming over his or her left shoulder so that the writing is not obscured by the thumb knuckle. Some left-handers may need to hold the pencil a little further from the point than right-handers. The authors also suggest that left-handers sit on a higher chair to prevent the elbow from locking into the side of the body when the writing has reached only half-way across the page.

The language of writing

Cripps and Cox recommend that teachers always use letter-names and not the sounds when giving writing instruction. Also, writing-related concepts should be taught, and these include: top, bottom, up, down, round, over, back, letter, word, pattern, left, right, join, curved, straight, tall, short, long, horizontal, diagonal (some useful mathematical concepts there!). Sassoon stresses the need for children to have consistent terminology used throughout the school, though in the early years children can invent their own words, for some of the aspects of handwriting. (For example, exit strokes may be called tails, flicks or kicks.) The importance of oral work has already been referred to (see page 94 regarding the formation of the letter 'g'). Some descriptively named groupings used by teachers include: the one o'clock club whose letters are formed by moving in an anti-clockwise direction (c, o, a, g, d, q), the down-back-up-again group (h, r, p, m, n, b, k), the stick team (j, i, x, z). Note that Cripps and Cox suggest teaching letters according to 'route' formation and not according to alphabetical sequence, though Sassoon's sequence and grouping of letters is somewhat different. She suggests: i, l, t, u, y, j; r, n, m, h, b, p, k; c, a, d, g, q, o, e; v, w, x, z and s, f.

Broadly speaking, i l t u y j   are formed by simple downward strokes and are downward strokes followed by a 'swing';

r n m h b p k begin with a down stroke followed with what may be termed a 'bridge'; c a d g q o e are characterised by clockwise curves; V W X Z are diagonally straight lines; s f are in no special group.

The early stages of handwriting

Cripps and Cox give many examples of children's pattern work (formal and informal) on pages 53–7 of their book. They emphasise the importance that some of the pattern work be done by children on the vertical plane and not solely on the horizontal. Desk tops are very useful for creating patterns in a large dimension. Later, the children should reach a stage where patterns (which should have some similarity to the shapes of letters) may be drawn using a pencil or felt-tip pen.

Later again, the majority of flowing letters should be formed in such a way that the writing implement is not lifted while a letter is being written and finishes in a position where logical joining strokes may follow naturally at a further stage. Decisions should be made regarding which letters to join, and then the ligatures should be taught and practised until they become automatic. It is not, however, necessary to wait until all letters have been taught in order to practise letter strings, for example: ca, en, at. As these letter strings are also part of our spelling system, the links with spelling are made. One of the first words that most children want to write is their own name (preferably in a simple sentence). Cripps and Cox suggest that children use their names to develop an interest in words and spelling. For example: Jason - as - on - son - so. Similarly, Sassoon refers to teachers of handwriting who always start with the letters in a child's name.

Writing from memory

As was stated in Chapter 3, Charles Cripps' ideas on the teaching of spelling coincide almost exactly with those of Margaret Peters and thus it is not surprising that Cripps and Cox stress the visual aspect of spelling stating that children:

> . . . must be taught to look closely at letters and letter strings, such as: ag, ere, ain, ome, etc, and then to write them without reference to the original image. (1990, p. 61)

Like Peters, they recommend the Look/Cover – Write/Check method of learning letter strings and spellings. I assume that the avoidance of copying applies to all (or most) of the work which children are asked to reproduce from 'models' and that they are taught to study manageable sections of texts to be copied, which are then written from memory. I assume, too, that checking over the finished product for errors is taught as part of the children's strategy in becoming responsible for their own correctness in spelling, punctuation, etc.

Interestingly too, Cripps and Cox point out (p. 18) that though the National Curriculum does not relate handwriting directly to spelling, the Bullock Report (1975) did point out such a relationship:

> The child can progress to letter groups with a variety of ligatures again in common use, such as: tion, ous, ttle, and ough. Practice with these not only helps to develop speed but has the advantage of reinforcing common spelling patterns.

The National Curriculum's statement is less explicit:

> As they become familiar with the conventions of writing, they should begin to learn spelling patterns. Pupils should be taught how to spell words which exemplify regular spelling patterns.

Cripps and Cox conclude by summarising some of the main requisites of teachers wishing to persuade colleagues to a change in school policy. These are:

1 A well-developed pre-writing programme that does not rush children into writing too early.

2 A great deal of discussion about the structure of words.

3 The introduction of flowing separate letters, followed by the joining of letter strings from the beginning.

4 A structured approach to teaching these skills to ensure correct letter formation from the start.

5 A strong emphasis at the outset on the writing of letters and words from memory.

Before concluding this chapter, I feel it both necessary and relevant to emphasise the fact that teachers should not stress the importance of handwriting and spelling at the *expense* of content in written work. Similarly, Beard (1984, p. 72) urges that the teaching of handwriting be kept in a reasonable perspective. He adds that it is possible for schools to give a disproportionate priority to the production and display of immaculately written and decorated pieces of writing which have an unimpressive content.

Teachers need to 'balance' their priorities giving thought to how children may be helped to produce work in which content has 'pride of place' but which, if it is to be published and/or displayed, is presented in a manner which gives status also to the children's handwriting and spelling. As Cripps and Cox state (p. 26) 'Handwriting *serves* writing' (my emphasis).

Summary

I think it worthwhile to reflect briefly on Peters' and Sassoon's views on handwriting and spelling. Peters undoubtedly sees a link between children's progress in spelling and correctly formed, speedy writing. As we have seen, her research indicated that children who had had plenty of practice in writing groups of letters in connected form evidenced both confidence and general correctness in their writing. We should remember, though, that her research involved 10-year-old children. Sassoon agrees that common letter sequences are useful when young children are learning to join letters. However, she considers that continuous writing may not be helpful to poor spellers, especially when writing long words. (Here I think she is referring to older children.) I think that continuous writing may be helpful in drawing the attention of poor spellers to the visual aspects of print and to common letter sequences within words, though (like Sassoon) I do not feel that writing *need* be continuous for the whole of words, especially long ones. I have never taught continuous writing to young children, but I do think that Sassoon's suggestions regarding baseline exit strokes may help to prepare them for continuous writing.

For obvious reasons, this chapter has not dealt *in detail* with the sequence in which letters may be taught, or letter formation, or the various handwriting styles. These are all matters which head-teachers and teachers need to discuss thoroughly and, of course, an important decision is the one regarding at which age joined handwriting should be taught. Among the many books which may prove useful are:

Cripps, C. (1988) *A Hand for Spelling*, LDA. (This book teaches handwriting and spelling together and contains over 500 photocopiable activities to take pupils from pre-writing skills through letter formation to spelling at an 11-year-old level.)

Sassoon, R. (1990) *Handwriting – the way to teach it*, Stanley Thornes Ltd. (The book covers all aspects of the subject including whole school planning and teaching letters in a practical sequence. Its aim throughout is to encourage flexibility and clear thinking about essential issues on the part of teachers.)

Smith, P. (1977) *Developing Handwriting*, Macmillan Education. (This is a highly illustrated book which makes clear to teachers what is available to them and their pupils in terms of writing styles, classroom materials, methods of instruction and practice. Peter Smith suggests that joined handwriting should commence in the first year of junior school.)

7 Effective teaching of spelling – the early years

Reference has already been made to the extremes which may exist in some schools with respect to the teaching of spelling. There can be a tendency in some schools to follow a rigid system, using books of spelling lists and 'rules' (even though there are very few spelling 'rules' which do not have a significant number of exceptions to them); in other schools, there can be a tendency to follow principles of spelling instruction which is said to be child-centred, and give instruction on an *ad hoc* occasional basis, with no real system for giving (or indeed detecting) remedial help to children with spelling difficulties. It is hoped to redress the balance between these two extremes.

Thus, the aim of this chapter is to give ideas for the gradual introduction of regular, and systematic spelling instruction which is based upon children's requirements (and, to some extent their choice). It also aims to promote children's interest in words and spelling and to ensure that all children experience success at their level of ability. Instruction recommended will generally be via a multi-sensory approach, and so although children's attention to the visual and motor aspects of print will be stressed (as urged by Schonell (1957) and Peters (1985)), attention will also be given to the auditory aspects of spelling and to accurate pronunciation. As Peters (1975) herself acknowledged:

> Obviously a child must be able to hear and discriminate letter sounds. Obviously too he must be able to articulate clearly. (p. 11)

Though we saw in Chapters 4 and 5 that most children's early writing ('invented spelling') reflected their awareness of symbol/sound correspondence in the writing process, this does not mean that all children understand this correspondence. Moreover, since Bryant and Bradley (1985, p. ix) have conducted research which indicates that children with spelling difficulties improve significantly when they are trained to categorise words by their sounds, especially with respect to alliteration and rhyme, it seems logical to use methods of instruction which may help to lessen (if not overcome) children's potential spelling difficulties.

We shall begin with consideration of the classroom environment in the reception class.

An environment for literacy

Since, broadly speaking, the literate adult is one who can read, write, speak and listen effectively, classrooms (and especially reception and infant classrooms) should reflect an atmosphere in which literacy as a whole is given status. This point is stressed by the National Curriculum's programme of study for reading as it recommends that young children should experience:

> . . . an environment in which they are surrounded by books and other reading material presented in an attractive and inviting way. The reading material should include material which is related to the real world, such as labels, captions, notices, children's newspapers, books of instructions, plans, maps, diagrams, computer print-out and visual display.
> (1990, p. 29)

It seems too that in a changing 'real world' some books displayed should represent ethnic minorities, even in classes where there are no children from ethnic minorities; there should also be some books which represent 'thinking' and 'strong' women. It is a good idea to include in class displays material brought in by the children themselves; this could include pictures, birthday and holiday cards and favourite books, thus establishing a link between home and school. This is particularly important for children whose first language is not English. Though Hall (1987) warns teachers against fading labels in classrooms, in my experience and that of many colleagues, most reception and infant classes are attractively and thoughtfully set out, and generally teachers score high marks for presentation, with labels and captions clearly and neatly labelled.

Ideally, the teacher's writing should be based on a whole school policy and presented in the style which the children will be expected to adopt, and about which the parents of children at the pre-school stage were informed. An area which appears to be overlooked in some classes is, however, the use that the children make of the material which surrounds them. Naturally, such use needs, in the first instances, to be stimulated by teachers. In order

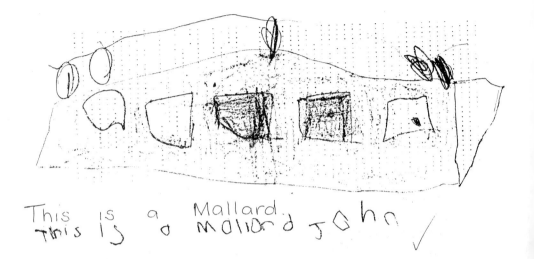

Figure 7.1 John's teacher had not discussed what *he* meant by 'Mallard'

to encourage children to interact with the literacy around them, there should be ongoing discussion about the material in the class, and particularly material which has been brought in by the children.

The development of children's vocabulary and their interest in literacy may be greatly promoted by regular and relevant class discussions which actively involve as many children as possible. As we have seen, verbal ability is often (though not always) highly correlated with children who become effective writers (Peters, 1985). I have included figure 7.1 to illustrate an occasion when, quite clearly, a teacher did not enter into discussion about the child's work, merely asking, 'What have you drawn, John?' John replied that he had drawn a mallard (he and his father were keen engine spotters and went to the nearby local station regularly). Obviously, the teacher did not realise that 'mallard' might also refer to trains since she took his paper, turned it upside down and wrote the caption for John to copy. He later told his mother, 'I tried to tell her it was the wrong way round, but she wasn't listening.'

I suppose we may feel sorry for the busy teacher, but what a waste of the child's knowledge and experience which could have been shared with other children (and presumably also the teacher!).

Differing pre-school experiences in literacy

As children commence school, it should be remembered that they will have had widely differing experiences, especially in terms of literacy and culture; thus, teachers have a vital role to play in helping children to bridge the gaps between their pre-school routines and experiences, and those which they will encounter in school. Factors relating to pre-school reading, writing, listening and speaking require very specific consideration by reception teachers in particular. For example, the child who has been regularly read to, talked to and generally made aware of the literacy around him or her (including his or her own name and address, 'labels' around the kitchen, printed words on television, street names, etc.) and who has been encouraged to experiment with 'writing' from an early age is likely to be also a good listener, with a mind which is both receptive and enquiring. This child is likely to feel 'at home' quite quickly in school and looking forward to extending his or her knowledge.

On the other hand, the child from a home in which literacy is given low status, or from a home in which English is the second language, is likely to feel very alien in a school situation in which he or she is surrounded by print and where he or she is expected to react to the 'strange', perhaps relatively formal language of the teacher. The teacher's first major job is to accept these children as they are, and where they are in terms of literacy; both respecting and developing whatever experiences they may have had so that gradually they are able to integrate into their new environment. Until they feel reasonably 'at home' it is unlikely that any real learning will take place.

The Kingman Report (1988) similarly made reference to differences in children's pre-school experiences (though it was concerned mainly with differences respecting Standard English):

> . . . when children go to school for the first time, their language may differ in many respects from Standard Engish depending on where they live, their parents' speech habits and so on. This is right and proper and a source of richness. (2.31)

Early handwriting instruction

The National Curriculum states that young children should be introduced to both upper and lower case letters in reception classes; thus, when taking into consideration children's varying levels of pre-school experience, it is important for teachers to be aware that many parents will have taught their children only capital letters, possibly because they are more easily formed and more easily differentiated. Smith's (1977) suggestions seem useful ones which may further help to bridge the gap between home and school.

> It is helpful to prepare a leaflet for parents, giving them some guidelines which can be handed to them as their children are enrolled. (p. 14)

As we have seen, many educationalists consider that teachers should encourage the correct formation of letters as soon as possible. Multi-sensory routines are recommended with, for example, children (in small groups) looking as the teacher demonstrates the formation of a letter, with the teacher talking about the formation of the letter while doing so. The children may then trace the letter in the air or on desks, copying the teacher's 'pattern'. Sandtrays, clay, plasticine, pastry, chalk and blackboards are all useful for reinforcing letter shapes. There is then the consideration as to whether or not teachers should encourage children to write 'freely' until all letters are being formed correctly (see Chapter 6 for Cripps' and Cox's and Sassoon's views on the subject). Cripps and Cox (1990) suggest various methods for recording children's ideas if correct letter formation has not been established (see pages 95–6). In any case, children's first names make ideal, relevant starting points for the introduction of letter formation and the function of upper and lower case letters (if the first letter is written as a capital). Moreover, children will see this exemplified if teachers of nursery and reception children use the children's first names on cloakroom hooks rather than (as is sometimes the case) allocating pictures to children to help them to identify their hook. Of course, if children find difficulty in identifying their names, then a picture of an object beginning with the initial letter of their name may be used alongside their name (for example, 'David' might be accompanied by an illustration of a drum). As soon as the child is able to identify his or her name, the illustration may be removed.

Using children's names in literacy encounters

Whether or not children can recognise their names as a 'whole', all children should benefit from being helped to pay close attention to the details of their names, especially the first letters; and teacher–child discussion about names (preferably in small groups) often provides an excellent introduction to one of the main uses of print. As we saw in Chapter 3, Peters (1985) recommended that children who can recognise their names be encouraged to develop an interest in language and words via associative learning using their names. Examples which I have used include:

> *T*racy likes (or does not like) *t*omatoes
> *A*nne likes (or does not like) *a*pples
> *P*eter has a *p*et
> *Ph*ilip likes *ph*otos.

Gradually, 'name sentences' may be extended, for example:

> *Sh*eila says she likes *sh*ops
> *J*ohn tells *j*okes and he *j*umps a lot.

(Interestingly, the unusual 'ohn' letter sequence originated from the Latin name, Johannes and the Hebrew name Yohanan, in which the letter 'h' was sounded.)

The examples given repeat the first letter/s of children's names, thus helping even very young children to be aware of alliteration and also the connection between sounds heard and their visual representation. However, such awareness should not be taken for granted simply because the *teacher* is aware of the connections; in many cases, awareness needs stimulation by explicit teacher/child discussion. 'Name sentences' may be constructed by groups of children and the teacher, who may then put the sentences in writing and place them above or below a picture or painting of themselves. Alternatively or additionally, 'name sentences' may be placed in alphabetical order so that alphabetical sequence is emphasised (learning the sequence of the alphabet will be discussed shortly). Naturally, children whose mother tongue is not English should have their first names written in their first language (this may require the involvement of the child's parents) followed by their 'name sentence' in English.

Peter's suggestions (1985) for helping children to become aware of words within their names (for example, 'Timothy likes moths') is, I think, an activity which should *follow* the alliterative stage, and is, perhaps, most useful for children who have made some progress in the spelling and writing process.

Judith Botham (1990) suggested that children's names could be used to develop their awareness of literacy's functional purposes. She described a felt board upon which may be placed the felt-backed names of children staying for school dinner, those having sandwiches and those going home for dinner; they may be changed daily by the children themselves (and may involve some mathematical calculations regarding how many children are doing what at dinner time). First names may later be accompanied by surnames. I suggest that gradually, perhaps in their second year at school, the children become accustomed to placing their names in alphabetical order (surnames first) after several discussions regarding the usefulness of alphabetical sequencing, and relating it to telephone directories, class registers and dictionaries.

Learning the alphabet

The National Curriculum (1990) recommends that at level 1 of spelling attainment, pupils should be able to 'write some letter shapes in response to speech sounds and letter names' (1990, p. 17). At level 2, one of its recommendations is that pupils should 'show knowledge of the names and order of the letters of the alphabet' (1990, p. 17). A gradual knowledge of the sounds of all the letters of the alphabet is essential if children are to make deductions about sound/symbol correspondence in the reading and writing process. There is, however, varied opinion among schools regarding whether or not to teach the names of letters in the alphabet along with their sounds, or to teach letter names separately. Indeed, in Chapter four, it was noted by Goswami and Bryant (1990) that when young children know both the names and sounds of the letter in the alphabet, they sometimes become confused and will thus, for example, spell 'car' as 'cr' since the name of the letter 'r' is pronounced as 'ar'. However, since most parents teach the alphabetical names first (often instead of alphabetical sounds), many children will commence school knowing some, or all, of the names of letters. Further, alphabetical names are used when helping children to learn the sequence of the alphabet (essential for dictionary skills, telephone directory use, etc.). Moreover, knowledge of the alphabetical names is helpful when children begin to make deductions about the reading and writing process since in, for example, words such as s**o**, g**o**, b**e**, m**i**ght, r**i**de, **u**niform, the vowels in italics are given the sound of their alphabetical name. Even very young children may soon be helped to be aware that letters do not have 'static' values in terms of sound, and children's names often illustrate the options in the reading and writing process (**P**hilip and **F**iona or D**a**vid and D**a**niel. As Cashdan (1990) says:

> Knowing the ABC enables children to organise the multiple grapheme-phoneme correspondences which form the core of the reading system . . . Knowing the alphabet also makes it easier to write. (pp. 51–2)

Indeed, there is increasing evidence that a knowledge of letters and their names *plus* the ability to name them easily is a strong predictor of success in pre-readers, and a 'strong correlate of reading achievement among beginners' (Adams, 1990, p. 62). Adams goes on to say:

> There is evidence that a comfortable knowledge of the names of letters hastens children's learning about their sounds because it mediates their ability to remember the sounds. That is, if I, as a learner, know that this particular symbol is called *b*, then I can use that fact to help myself to remember that its sound is /b/. (p. 63)

Similarly, following a fairly recent study involving entrants to 33 ILEA infant schools, starting while they were still in the nursery class, and following them through to the end of infant school, Barbara Tizard (1988) found:

> The number of letters that children could identify before they started school was the strongest predictor of their Young's reading score at seven and a half. The extent to which parents read aloud to their children, both pre-school and during infant school was also related to their reading skills, but much less strongly. (p. 11)

Tizard's last sentence suggests that the provision of a literary environment (though desirable) is not, on its own sufficient to ensure the child's development in literacy (see, too, Mudd, 1989). Explicit information regarding letter names (and sounds) is, it seems, essential for many children in order to ensure their literacy *progress* (Ehri, 1991). I would suggest that children be taught alphabet names and sounds separately in the very early stages of instruction, but that the two be related to each other fairly soon (depending, of course, on the child's progress in these areas).

In classrooms, letters of the alphabet (plus illustrations depicting their sound) should be placed at eye-level; some reception classes have their alphabetical display at a level of 5 feet or more and they seem to serve more as a 'window dressing' than as a functional part of literacy which is constantly referred to by both children and teacher. The children's 'name sentences' may also be placed above or below the appropriate letter of the alphabet; much depends on the space available to the teacher. If 'name sentences' are placed near the letters of the alphabet, it is likely that some letters will not be accompanied by a child's name. In such cases, the names of children's pets or toys could be gradually added to the display.

Difficult letters to represent in terms of sound are often found to be X and Y. I have found that words such as *explosion* and *exciting* are helpful, after, of course, their meanings have been discussed and they have been represented by relevant illustration. Letterland (1990) suggests words such as *box*, *fox*, *next*, *six* and names like *Max* and *Maxine*. With respect to the letter Y, I have found that words such as *yes, yellow, yoghurt* are helpful (if illustrated appropriately) and usually relevant. Names such as *Yolande* and *Yonna* may also be helpful (if somewhat unusual).

Teachers may have their own methods of helping children to learn the alphabet in sequence; one method which I have used successfully is via the tune of *The Happy Wanderer*, to which the letters of the alphabet may be sung.

I		love	to		go	
Oh		A	B		C	
a		wan-	der-		ing	
D		E	F		G	
a-long		the	moun-tain	track		
HI		J	K	L	M	
And		as	I		go	
N		O	P		Q	
I		like	to		sing	
R		S	T		U	
my		knapsack	on		my	back
V		W	X		Y	Z

Those familiar with the melody will appreciate the fact that its rhythm helps children to be aware of the rhyme which may be stressed on the letters 'C' (go) and 'G' (ing) and also the letters 'Q' (go) and 'U' (sing). As noted earlier, Bryant and Bradley (1985) lay stress on children's awareness of rhyme in helping them to develop reading and writing abilities. Singing the words of the song (which I always present in written form) followed by singing the letters of the alphabet on a regular basis, can help children to learn the alphabet painlessly and with enjoyment. Also, in the early stages, teachers may take the letters and the words of the song in 'slow motion' while they point to the letters of the words in sequence, thus emphasising the left-to-right sequence of print. This is a fact which is not necessarily obvious to children, especially those whose pre-school experiences have been limited. In fact, some adults who attend classes in adult basic education in order to learn to read are unsure of the left-to-right sequence of print, and many who attend classes to improve writing skills do not know all the letters of the alphabet in sequence. Often they are able to recall the alphabet's beginning and end, but are very hazy about eight or nine letters in the middle. This, of course, makes the use of dictionaries a very slow process until the alphabet has been learned correctly – and learning the alphabet may also be a very slow process since incorrect habits have been formed.

The 'I-spy' game, which is usually enjoyed by children of all ages (especially on rather long car journeys) may be helpful in giving children in the reception class alphabetic knowledge, particularly if teachers use letter names and also letter sounds. Moreover, the game may be varied so that children can take it in turns to 'spy' objects in alphabetical order, so that no sounds are omitted. Later, concentration may be on those letters whose sounds prove rather difficult for children, these usually include a, e, i, o, u (the vowels) and m, n, q, v, w, x, y. Similarly, the game 'I went to the supermarket and I bought apples, beans, crisps . . . ' (whereby children add on items purchased in alphabetical order), may help to reinforce their knowledge of letter sounds and alphabetical sequence.

As has been indicated, much of what has been discussed regarding children's early learning may be undertaken with the whole class of children and consolidated by work in small groups, where individual difficulties may be identified, noted (preferably in a record book) and remedied. My views on group work are in accordance with those of Smith (1977):

> One very common misunderstanding is that any instruction
> a teacher provides must be given to children individually.
> Some young teachers have been made to feel guilty if they
> fall short of this ideal by giving a lesson to a group . . .
> Indeed, the most economic use of a teacher's time in
> developing basic skills in children would seem to be through
> group work, for which children are grouped according to
> their needs, at least during part of the day. (p. xi)

Indeed, the recent report to the Secretary of State by Robin Alexander
et al. (DES, 1992), while acknolwedging the fact that there are times
when individual children need individual help, observes that however
skilled and energetic a teacher may be, each individual receives only a
minute proportion of the teacher's attention if the teacher tries to teach
individually on a regular basis (p. 28). They suggest that group work
can be successful provided that there are not too many groups working
on too many activities so that teachers are able to work 'purposefully with
each group' (p. 30). Moreover, they refer to whole class teaching, stating:

> Whole class teaching is associated with higher order
> questioning, explanations and statements, and these in
> turn correlate with higher levels of pupil performance.
> (p. 28)

The report's conclusion is that teachers need to strike a balance and apply
class, group or individual teaching according to the task in hand (p. 30).

Nursery rhymes

It was stated earlier in this chapter that a positive environment for literacy
is one in which the children are surrounded by a variety of 'literacy'
material which is used regularly. I should like to remind teachers of young
children of the value of traditional nursery rhymes in their regular reading
sessions with their children. There is some evidence from a study carried
out by the author in 1974 that fewer children are taught traditional rhymes
at home than, say, in the 1950s and earlier. Yet many of these rhymes
have strong rhythms as well as rhyme and alliteration, all of which young
children in particular respond to so readily. In my teaching experience, I
have found that the introduction of one traditional rhyme per week,
displayed in large writing at the children's eye level, is most useful in
encouraging children to enjoy language and in helping them to make

inferences about written text and reading. Many rhymes may be acted out by the children, and perhaps given more 'plot' by the teacher. For example, 'Who Killed Cock Robin?', 'Mary, Mary, Quite Contrary,' 'Old Macdonald Had A Farm', 'Here We Go Round The Mulberry Bush', 'Polly Put The Kettle On', and 'Hickory, Dickory Dock', are all suitable for acting out and most of them have simple melodies. Dramatic activities help to develop children's imagination as well as their recall of events; discussion of rhymes may include references to children's names within the class and the meanings of words. Thus, the rhyme 'Mary, Mary' could include teacher–child discussions which will help to develop reasoning skills which are closely related to reading and writing (Thorndike, 1917). It is likely, too, that when children go home and recite nursery rhymes, their parents and/or grandparents will be able to join in the recitation and possibly even produce their childhood rhyme books. Thus, the enjoyment of books may be shared by families and provide a further link between home and school. All this is not to say, however, that the many modern and beautifully illustrated books of verse should be ignored; the plea is simply to balance contemporary verse/rhymes with traditional forms from the past.

Early 'play' writing

The point at which reception children undertake writing tasks will, of course, depend on whether or not it is the school's policy to wait for children to achieve correct letter formation before they write independently. In its programme of study for writing, the National Curriculum suggests that 'play' writing should encourage pupils in a wide range of activities; it goes on to list some examples: a playhouse, class shop, office, hospital. Jennie Foster (1991) recommends a café (plus menus and price lists), a launderette (plus instructions for different machines, soap powder, advertisements and warnings of danger) and a space capsule (plus charts, maps, lists of equipment, lists of telephone numbers, computer instructions, and safety rules) as unusual stimuli for young children's writing experiences.

Similarly, Hall (1987a, p. 89) refers to a nursery class which played at running a puppet theatre. Hall's descriptions of the work and writing involved sounds very exciting and includes the children making programmes, tickets, posters and seating plans. All these ideas are potentially stimulating as they engage children in writing activities involving functional and purposeful literacy. Again, though, a note of caution is required, particularly with respect to inexperienced teachers. A class of busy children engaged in a variety of activities *may* be masking children who need specific help in some area; Alexander *et al.* (DES, 1992, p. 29) stated that teachers should not have too many groups of pupils working on too many different activities. Moreover, it should be remembered that Lambley (1992) referred to some teachers feeling unsure about their competence to teach the basic subjects after inadequate training at college.

In Chapter 6, reference was made to the fact that young children, who are encouraged to write in any way that they can (irrespective of correct letter formation) in order that their desire to write is not inhibited, may, in fact, encounter problems later on in school. Once habits are formed (especially incorrect habits) they are much more difficult to correct. This is evident among the many adults in basic education centres who reveal idiosyncratic letter formation and often write words containing a mixture of capital letters and lower case letters. Additionally, research regarding the correlation between children's progress in reading and their knowledge of letter names and sounds (Ehri (1991) and Adams (1990)) suggests that teachers of young children should also be paying attention to promoting such knowledge, as well as promoting a stimulating literacy environment for them. It seems of limited value to arouse children's interest in literacy and their desire to write if, after a year or two, some of them have to re-learn letter formation and begin to learn about our reading/writing system.

Naturally, the experienced teacher will not only be able to stimulate children to learn through interesting 'play' projects, but they will also be able to keep a watchful eye out for children with difficulties of whatever nature. I think, as in many areas of life, what is required is a balance of experiences: thus informal learning activities should be complemented by more formal and structured teaching methods which help the teacher to monitor individual children more easily, and may also, depending on the teacher's ingenuity, be equally stimulating for the children.

Early spelling instruction

Peters (1985), Schonell (1942) and Smith (1977) are among the many educationalists who believe that the early detection of difficulties is the key to prevention of serious difficulties in the junior school. It is thus intended to consider some of the more structured methods by which young children may be helped to develop their knowledge about our spelling system. While acknowledging the fact that children generally begin school with widely differing literacy experiences, it is suggested that spelling instruction may be given when they are able to write their own names and have evidenced some understanding regarding the relationship between the sounds of the alphabet and the written symbols which represent them, albeit an approximate representation in some instances. (Such understanding is likely to have been facilitated by means of activities such as the ones referred to earlier in this chapter.) It is helpful, too, if children are able to form most (or all) the letter shapes correctly when spelling instruction begins. Thus, the more practice that children have had in making letter shapes (in clay, sand, plasticine, the air, or on 'touch' material such as velvet or sandpaper), the more likely that correct letter shapes will be learned. Unfortunately, it is not unusual to find that some junior children still have difficulties in forming their letters, and some still confuse certain letters. It is useful to have many boxes of letters available, not only for playing with, but also in order that children who find difficulty in letter formation can still participate actively in spelling instruction.

Broadly speaking, the aims of early spelling instruction are the encouragement of positive attitudes towards writing and spelling and the building of confidence via success.

The use of rhyme in early reading/spelling instruction

The use of nursery rhymes has already been referred to, and these also provide excellent models upon which teachers may base their early spelling instruction without detracting in any way from the children's enjoyment of the rhymes (provided that instruction is brief and in 'small steps'). In the early stages, teachers may decide to discuss only one line of a rhyme with the children. It is often a good idea for the children to work in groups, according to their development in the reading/writing process, with each group working on the same rhyme which has been chosen by the class as a whole. While waiting for the teacher to give them attention, the children may be illustrating their chosen rhyme or carrying out some other activity. Teachers may use the board or large sheets of white paper, or overhead projectors to illustrate salient features of the line (or lines) to be discussed with each group.

In the example which follows, the instruction suggested is quite detailed; the detail is included simply to give teachers some idea of the extent of instruction which may be extracted from one line of rhyme. Teachers should include only instruction which they consider to be relevant to their children and should bear in mind the maxim 'a little and often'.

Thus, for example, in the first line of 'Humpty Dumpty' teachers may, with the children's co-operation, draw attention to the similarities between 'Hump' and 'Dump', perhaps repeating both letter names and letter sounds, and looking carefully at the formation of the letter string 'ump'. Teachers may also demonstrate with plastic letters how 'Hump' may be converted into 'Dump' by simply replacing the letter 'H' with the letter 'D'. The blend of 'ty' and its 'ti' sound may be a useful example of a *fairly* common letter blend, for example: dirty, empty, plenty, twenty. Perhaps there are children or teachers in the class or school with 'ty' in their names, for example, Rafferty or Haggarty; there is also the first line of 'Hickety, Pickety, my Black Hen', which repeats the 'ty' blend.

In considering the words 'Hump' and 'Dump' and then adding on the 'ty' sound, the words have been divided into two syllables. Schonell (1942) disapproved of the division of words since he felt that it distorted the actual pattern (or schema) of the word. However, like Todd (1982), I feel that division of words into syllables is sometimes useful, but also like Todd, I think that putting in lines to divide a word (Hump/ty) does distort the image of the word for the novice reader or writer.

The use of capital letters for 'Humpty' and 'Dumpty' may be noted and related to the use of capitals for the children's names; moreover, if any of the children's first or surnames begin with 'H' or 'D', then this too may be commented upon and the name/s displayed in writing by the teacher (or the child) beneath 'Humpty' or 'Dumpty'.

Discussion of the word 'sat' may include looking at the word and common letter blend 'at' within 'sat'. The letters 'at' may be written on the board or paper, or formed using plastic letters, then the teacher and children may try to form other words by placing other letters in front of the blend, for example: fat, hat, mat, pat, rat. In this way, children may be introduced to word blends and 'families'. Also, if children say the words formed aloud, they may realise that they rhyme and begin to understand what is meant when we talk about rhyme.

The word 'a' is generally recognised by all children for whom English is their first language; teachers may also wish to ask children to recall the alphabetical name for this letter.

A useful contrast is provided if the word 'wall' is discussed since it is irregular in terms of sound/symbol correspondence. Again, teachers may isolate the sound (and word) 'all' and, using the board, paper or plastic letters, demonstrate how it may be transformed into, for example: ball, call, fall (which occurs in the second line of the rhyme), hall, tall. And, again, children may be encouraged to form the words in writing or using plastic letters. This, too, illustrates how words which are visually (and aurally) similar may be placed into 'families'.

To conclude the instruction, teachers may revise briefly what has been discussed in the lesson, and remind the children (by demonstration) about correct letter formation. If the group of children then form the letters in the air, the teacher may be able to identify any children with specific difficulties and help them before moving on to the next group of children. The group which has just received instruction may reproduce in writing or plastic letters the line studied beneath their illustration of it. This is a good opportunity to help children to acquire the habit of writing from memory, but it needs very careful and constant guidance. I suggest that a *variation* of the Look/Cover – Write/Check method (see page 40) should be used to help young children to avoid 'blind' copying. Thus, children may be encouraged to look at a whole word, say the whole word, repeat its letter names (in left-to-right sequence) and finally try to write the word from memory. Some children will be able and ready to check against the original spelling for accuracy; others will need more experience before they are able to monitor their own writing. Since the teacher and the group have discussed and 'analysed' the line of rhyme together, attempting to write out the line from memory is not usually too difficult, although it should be pointed out that training in the amended 'Look/Cover – Write/Check' method should not be given at the same time as the instruction in reading and spelling since this will almost certainly overload the children's learning tasks. Such training may be undertaken when children are learning to write their names from memory. Moreover, I consider that children who are not able to recall word patterns from memory should, in the early stages, be allowed to copy work.

The whole lesson may be brought full circle by a class reading of the rhyme from the wall display and, perhaps, some drama centred on the rhyme. During the preceding lesson, the children may have been actively involved in discussion, thought and prediction. Moreover, they may have had their attention drawn to visual and auditory aspects of words and word parts (possibly irregular as well as regular). They may also have read aloud, reproduced text (either in writing or in plastic letters) and been involved in some dramatic activity. By these methods they should have learned a great deal about reading, writing and language in a lesson relevant to their needs and ability, culminating in a 'fun' activity.

For instruction to be effective, teachers should consolidate the lesson by revising the instruction the next day, or as soon as possible, with the children participating actively in the lesson recall; structure will be maintained if further instruction (possibly the second line of the rhyme) is related to what has already been discussed. Thus, the teacher's records of letters, words and word 'families' studied is vital.

Of course, teachers may prefer to make their early spelling instruction relevant to a class project, and thus, for example, the sentence, 'We are going to make a post office' could be studied in a similar way with 'we' 'are' and 'to' providing three common but irregular words for some children to learn; 'office' could provide an example of words within a word (off – ice), and the letters 'ing' could provide an example of a very common letter string; it could be considered along with other words containing the same 'family'. For example: going, making, taking and, perhaps later, sing, spring, sting, etc. In projects on post offices, many teachers have found that a class post box is very useful for stimulating children to write, and if children complain because they cannot read each other's letters, it seems an ideal time to explain that this is why we need to learn about spelling in order to understand each other's writing easily. However, teachers should ensure that all the children receive letters.

Letter blends in names

The importance and relevance of children's names in the reading and writing process has already been noted. They may be further used to develop children's awareness of common letter blends and digraphs. (A digraph is one sound made up of two letters; blends occur when the letters that represent two or three distinct sounds are pronounced closely together. Thus, *ch* is a digraph but *st* is a blend.) For example, *ch* – Cheryl, Charles, Richard; *sh* – Sheila, Shaun (if there is a Sean in the class, his name may be used to help children to realise that not all words are spelled according to sound); *st* – Stella, Steven, Stephen; *th* – Elizabeth, Timothy, Heather; *wh* – White, Whittaker; *ph* – Philip, Phyllis, Stephen (though *ph* has a 'v' sound in the latter name). The relevant letters may be underlined or printed above the children's 'name sentences' in a different colour. Naturally, the sequence in which these digraphs or blends are taught depends upon the children's needs and upon related class activities. Thus, the blend 'st' may be related to the word 'post' in a class engaged in organising a post office. During teacher/child discussions, other words containing the 'st' blend may be identified, such as step, star, stop, last, lost. These may be written on the board by the teacher and instruction may involve articulating the words, looking at them carefully in written form (perhaps with the 'st' underlined) thus emphasising the child's visual and auditory learning, for example, '**St**ephen is going to **st**op in the po**st** office.' Studying the words in a meaningful context helps children to see spelling as part of the writing process, and not just something represented by lists of words. When children are able to do so, they may be encouraged to put such sentences, and their 'name sentences' into written form.

Children's early writing

By the end of their first year in school, and certainly during their second year, many children will be producing written work which reflects their deductions about our spelling system (invented spelling), and which includes a reasonable number of words in traditional orthography, spelled from memory and including their names and addresses. This is what Temple *et al.* (1988, p. 74) call *transitional* spelling since spelling errors are becoming more influenced by learning and less by intuition. Hannovy (1991) suggests that after four terms in school, most children will be able to write at least six words, correctly spelled, from memory. Of course, some children will be able to recall more than six words; it is those children who are able to recall less than, say, four words who may need specific help with their spelling. I suggest too that, like Hannovy, teachers construct their own screening tests early during the children's second year in school to check attitudes to literacy, and any difficulties related to auditory perception and perceptuo-motor ability, so that help may be given as soon as possible. (Suggestions for meeting special needs are given in Chapter 9.)

Use of spelling resources

At this stage, children should be made aware of the variety of resources which they can use when they need help with spelling. Although the teacher is an important 'resource', I feel strongly that children should not spend time queuing to ask the teacher to enter a required word into their personal dictionaries, and which is often 'overlooked' when the child requires the word again. Apart from the noise which is frequently synonymous with children queuing, there is seldom any real learning taking place if the child simply copies the word from the dictionary on to his or her work. In Chapter 4, Graves' methods of encouraging children to write were discussed; he advises teachers to establish set 'rules' during writing periods. Similarly, I consider that even quite young children may be taught to observe simple 'rules' if they are explained carefully so that the children understand their purpose. Thus, I suggest that teachers make it a rule that children do not go out to the teacher for spellings, instead they may be encouraged to make use of a variety of spelling resources (which, of course, include the teacher, who is generally the most valuable spelling resource and counsellor that the children have). The following suggested spelling resources may be useful to teachers of young children.

Teachers

It is suggested that teachers move round the desks systematically with their notebook which records individual difficulties or successes, ensuring that no child is overlooked. If recording is not done almost immediately, it is likely that much important information about the child's work will be forgotten. As the teacher stops at a desk (or set of desks), children there may ask for words that they need. If the word is needed before the teacher arrives to give help, children may be given two main options: they may write only the first letter or first and last letters of a word required, leaving a space for the middle of the word; thus, if a child requires the word 'steam' he or she may write 's----' or 'st--m', or he or she may attempt to write the whole word as he or she thinks it should be written. The former strategy usually has the advantage of preventing the child from reinforcing an incorrect spelling (and it is generally the less able speller who chooses that strategy), while the second strategy may give the teacher an insight into whether the child's spelling miscues indicate a fairly good spelling strategy, or whether they indicate some confusion about the spelling system. Once teachers arrive at the desk, and are asked for spellings by individual children, they may enter the required spelling into the child's personal, alphabetically-sequenced dictionary which the child has opened at the appropriate letter of the alphabet. If the child tried to write the whole word (rather than the first and last letters), then the teacher may underline the part of the word which was incorrect. For example, if the child wrote 'stem' or 'steem' for 'steam', the teacher may underline the letters 'ea' in the child's dictionary (with the child watching all the time). The word, similarly underlined, may also be written in the margin of the child's book near to the misspelling. When the child finishes his or her work, it may then be a routine matter (but remember that routines need careful and regular reinforcement) for the child, using the Look/Cover – Write/Check method (see page 40) to write any new spellings in the margin below those of the teacher, and also above his or her own version of the spelling in the text. His or her incorrect spelling of the word may be neatly crossed out with one line. It may be remembered (Chapter 3) that Peters (1985) encouraged children to rub out incorrect spellings and replace them with the correct ones. Like Todd (1982), I consider that the incorrect spellings may serve as a useful guide to the child's spelling strategies.

Training children to look carefully at words and to cover words so that they are not copied, and to check for accuracy, may be time consuming at first, but if reinforced regularly, the method soon becomes second nature, and helps these young children to begin to become responsible for their own learning. Moreover, their personal dictionaries represent a valuable source of information about the child's vocabulary and his or her spelling difficulties since, if any words are entered several times, they indicate that the words are ones used frequently by the child and also that they have not been learned effectively. Thus, teachers may make a note of such words alongside the child's name in their record books and use them for individual work with the child (or a group of children with similar problems).

Word charts

A further spelling resource for young children may be word charts, perhaps placed just above any alphabetical charts in the classroom (though some teachers may prefer them to be kept separate from other alphabetical charts). The design of the word chart may follow Jennifer Walton's suggestions for busy teachers in a leaflet entitled 'How can I find the time?' (produced by the United Kingdom Reading Association, 1988). She acknowledges that charts with high-frequency or topic-related words are not a new idea, but points out that they are quick to make and easily accessible to the child. She suggests a grid with ten rows down and five columns across, in which the rows are numbered (1–10); the columns have a square of coloured paper at the head of each column. Her example is:

	Green paper	Yellow paper	Red paper
1	in	was	is
2	I	he	it
3	up	yes	no
↓			
10			

Walton writes that the more proficient children will scan, find and use the words, or use it as a spelling check. The less able child may also try this method, or be given additional help, for example: 'The word you want is in the red column', or 'Look along row 3', or even 'It's on row 3 and in the red column.' I consider that the skills used in scanning for words, and in using a matrix format to do so, are ones which may prepare children well for more sophisticated scanning techniques, often advocated (but seldom taught or used effectively) in junior and secondary schools. My suggested alternative to Walton's chart is one in which three charts are used, each containing some of the letters of the alphabet in sequence. The first has ten columns across displaying the letters A–J, the second has ten columns for the letters K–T and the third needs only six columns for the letters U–Z. The number of columns down may be as Walton suggests, five in number – it all depends on the teacher, the children and the wall-space available. Like Walton, I think that word charts for young children are perhaps best used for high-frequency words rather than topic-related words since the latter will obviously change regularly. I suggest that the high-frequency words are placed in alphabetical order in the vertical columns so that more able spellers may be introduced to dictionary skills at an early age. For example:

	A	B	C	D	E → J
1	all	back	call	day	each
2	am	be	can	did	Easter
3	an	big	cap	do	egg
4	are	but	car	does	empty
5	at	by	cat	don't	ever

If velcro is placed on the squares, and the words are put on velcro-backed cards, easy change of word positions is facilitated. The words shown on these cards are related to the needs of young children with whom I have worked; naturally, teachers will include words relevant to their children. I suggest a gradual increase of words on the chart, with frequent class and group discussions of new words. Teachers may also use the charts as a game whereby the class, or groups, may (after explicit demonstration by the teacher) locate words for themselves. For example, questions may include: 'What is the word in column H across and 4 down?' If the child locates the word and is able to read it corectly, the next question might be: 'Can you spell it without looking at it again?' or, alternatively, 'Can you spell it after you have looked at it for 5 (or more) seconds?'

Such games help to familiarise children with the words in the chart and facilitate their speedy location. Depending on the size of writing on the chart, the children may need to move closer to the chart to locate a required word and, of course, they may ask other children's help if locating words proves difficult for them. An overall rule may be that the children look carefully at the words and then write them without referring to the chart, but checking, of course, that their recalled spelling is correct.

Word banks

A third suggested spelling resource for children is in the form of word banks. Naturally, many teachers have their own ideas for such 'banks'; I have found that they are most successful and durable if thick card, or card covered by removable plastic covers, is used. Postcard-sized cards, which may be stored in a small box, usually work quite well, and individual boxes may be supplied to tables or groups of children. These word banks may be used for topic-related words and words related to the needs of particular children on a table or in a group. Walton (1988) suggests that 30 cards work well, one card for each letter, plus one for the consonant digraphs, ch, sh, th, wh; she also adds that more sophisticated groups might need a card for ph. (I have found that the 'qu' blend is useful too.) Again, children who share word banks may help each other with the location of words required and, of course, the children will need constant reminders about trying to visualise words required rather than merely copying them. Many children will also need regular reminders about handling cards carefully, and replacing them in alphabetical order. (If the cards have holes punched in them, they may be placed on a ring so that the alphabetical order is retained.)

Walton reminds teachers that resources such as word banks and word charts need regular 'maintenance'. She urges teachers to check that children do still need the same words, revising charts and index cards. Some teachers use word banks instead of personal dictionaries, but I consider that the child needs both, since the former represents a more 'communal' collection of words, whereas the latter is obviously personal to one child and, as has been stated, words repeated several times in a personal dictionary will help teachers to be aware that a word is causing specific difficulties and thus supply appropriate remediation.

Class picture dictionaries

Further and attractive resources are easy-to-use picture dictionaries which may be used for browsing as well as for locating words. Perhaps there could be one or two for each table or group and, perhaps, these could also vary in difficulty, especially with respect to the size of print and number of entries.

As with most resources, children need careful and regular training in their use so that positive (good) habits are formed in the children's early years. In order to facilitate effective dictionary use, it is a good idea to have sets of letters of the alphabet (plastic ones are usually quite durable) which small groups of children may be asked to present in sequence, possibly using the melody of 'The Happy Wanderer' to aid them. When children are able to do this fairly easily, it may be a good idea to introduce the idea of speedy sequencing in the form of a game. Thus, a group may be told: 'That was very good and you managed to do it while the class counted 30' (etc). However, less able children should never be made to feel that they are failures, and should only be timed once the teacher is sure that they will achieve a count which they will consider to be a mark of success.

Children should be reminded, too, that of all the class resources for spelling, their own personal dictionaries are very valuable, and thus their use should be second nature to them. (Unfortunately, in some schools, children's personal word books seem to be used only by the teacher!)

Teachers' oral reactions to children's written work

In the earliest stages of the writing process, teachers usually move round the class, giving 'on the spot' help where necessary. Discussion about children's drawings and their content is vital in placing primary importance on their intended communication rather than upon their actual presentation (Graves, 1983). Such discussion, especially when undertaken within small groups, will generally reveal too the children's personal levels of language and their language needs. As Moyle (1982) states, children's normal language usage and the development of their concepts of word meaning:

> . . . tend to be more obvious within group discussion than individual conversations between teacher and child. (p. 52)

Marking written work

As children become more fluent in expressing themselves in writing, teachers will not only interact orally with children regarding their work, but also help them to improve work, giving attention to content as well as to spelling and handwriting difficulties. Children may be asked by teachers to read their own work aloud rather than teachers attempting to read the work themselves. The advantages of this method are mainly two-fold: firstly, it places emphasis on the content of the work rather than on spelling, handwriting, etc; and, secondly, young authors can generally interpret any spelling miscues in their writing more easily than an adult, and significant pauses are often made in the reading by the young author which generally make the text more comprehensible. (Young writers often omit punctuation and adults may need to read work several times in order to comprehend their texts fully.) After the reading, teachers may like to comment orally on the work as a whole, referring, for example, to its positive qualities as a piece of written communication (Well sequenced? Exciting? Descriptive? Humorous? etc.). Secondary evaluation may be concerned with handwriting, spelling, the correct use of capital letters, grammar and, possibly, punctuation (depending upon the child's stage of writing development). Since this book is concerned mainly with spelling, it is intended to discuss only how teachers may react to misspellings and/or evidence of progress in spelling rather than any of the other factors mentioned above.

Naturally, children should be given praise for any spellings which they have apparently learned recently. Such progress is usually easy to observe if teachers refer to their own records and also to the child's personal dictionary while marking work. Like Peters (1985) I think that if a child has, for example, ten spelling errors, then only three or four of these should be corrected (and discussed), and these should be spellings of importance/relevance to the child. (However, if the work is to be rewritten for display, children will generally see the importance of correcting all, or most, of their errors so that work is easily understood by those who read it, but only three or four of the important relevant misspellings need to be *learned* by the child.) Correct spellings may be written in the margin and the child's personal dictionary and, as was stated earlier, children should be in the habit of writing the correct version of the spelling below the teacher's writing in the margin and also above their own misspelling, which they may cross out neatly. The Look/Cover – Write/Check method should be used for such corrections. If a child is constantly misspelling the same words, then specific remedial action is called for. (Remedial methods will be discussed in the chapter on children with spelling difficulties.)

A further, important part of teachers' interaction with children's work is their remark on the work. It is still common practice in some schools for teachers to write: 'Very good', or 'Well done', or 'You must try harder with your writing' at the end of children's work. Such comments are not helpful in enabling the child to understand why a piece of writing was (or was not) successful; moreover, they do not give individual status to the child's writing. I think that the teacher's initial oral comments to the child regarding the content of his or her work, may also be expressed in writing to illustrate to the child that his or her work is valued by the teachers, and also to give some permanence to the teacher's evaluation.

There are, of course, some children who produce one or two sides of writing which cannot be read easily (even by the child) since their spellings are so bizarre. (I recall several students on teaching practice wondering how best to help such children.) In these cases, I think that teachers may 'gently' explain that written communication needs to be understood; they may then work with the child to try to 'decipher' one or two lines of writing and suggest that on future occasions the child works with them (or an adult helper who understands the 'writing philosophy' of the school). Wedell (1974, p. 61) urges teachers to let children who experience writing difficulties, for whatever reason, use tapes of oral speech to express ideas they wish to convey without stress. Adults may then transfer ideas expressed by such children to paper for the children to see and to read (with the adult's help) and possibly to copy out (perhaps just a sentence or two, under supervision). Naturally, such children will probably need specific remedial help; this will be discussed in the chapter on children with spelling difficulties.

Informal testing

The idea of testing young children at all (albeit informally) may be regarded by some teachers with horror – as evidenced by the outcry of some teachers against the suggestions for testing young children made in the National Curriculum. Yet, in my experience, provided that the teacher ensures that no children are humiliated or made to feel failures, children enjoy monitoring their own progress and seeing tangible proof of success. Nothing succeeds like success. It is therefore essential that children are grouped according to their abilities when informal tests are undertaken, and tests are likely to be given only in year 2. These young children are more likely to succeed if they are encouraged to become responsible for choosing words to be learned. They may, for example, choose words related to topic work, or words which interest them as individuals.

Moseley (1974) and Todd (1982) have observed that some children, and boys in particular, may have a negative attitude to spelling; such children may like to select names of 'pop' stars, football players, etc., for their chosen learning. Children may be grouped broadly into three bands; those of above average spelling ability, those of average spelling ability and those of below average spelling ability. The division into bands or groups should not cause any problems if done in a sensitive manner and in conjunction with how the children feel about their spelling abilities. Some adults find it quite surprising that even young children are able to judge their approximate levels within a class; and, of course, children may always decide to join another group of higher or lower ability. Usually, I allow children to choose names of colours or nearby districts to identify their groups. The number of words to be learned per week may vary from two to eight, according to ability and the children's suggestions within the group. I found that a good time for groups to select their words was in a 10-minute period on Monday afternoons prior to the reading of the current story. Sometimes, chosen words were names of characters in the story. (In my opinion, the most important consideration is to have a routine for such activities to which the children become accustomed.)

Once words had been selected by the groups, I wrote them on the board and discussed briefly any interesting and/or unusual characteristics of one or two words with all the class. After the children had gone home, it did not take long for me to write the words to be learned in their dictionaries with a symbol 'L' at the side to denote that they were to be learned. Todd (1982) recommends that teachers also write the children's personal spellings on paper placed in envelopes so that they may be taken home to learn. This may be a good idea in some cases, but I must add a cautionary note since I consider it vital that parents should first understand the philosophy of the school regarding the Look/Cover – Write/Check method of spelling, and more importantly, they should not become impatient with the child so that learning becomes a hated task. If there is any danger of the latter eventuality, then I prefer to help the children to do their learning at school (and we should remember that for some children, learning new spellings presents very few problems).

My next task on the Monday evening was to put the selected words into sentences, combining them with high-frequency words which the children had been using in their work. Thus, if the class had been involved in a project on pets and the above average group had included: important, clean, regular, cages, feline and canine in their words to be learned, I might have constructed three sentences such as 'We have been talking about pets. It is important to clean their cages regularly. A cat may be called a feline friend, and a dog may be called a canine friend.' These sentences combine new spellings, new vocabulary, high-frequency words and a reinforcement of the meaning of the new vocabulary. (The book on grammar by Cornwell (1878), see page 29, may seem rather 'heavy' and uninspiring to the modern eye, but its linkage of exercises on grammatical knowledge to general knowledge, probably ensured that the children had quite a good store of general facts, albeit at a surface level).

If the group of average spellers had included 'clean' and 'cage' in their words to be learned, I might have constructed a sentence such as 'We are going to clean out the cages of our pets each day.'

For the below average spellers, who might have chosen to learn the spellings 'Manchester' or 'Everton' (or other names), I might have constructed sentences such as: 'I like to see Everton play' or 'I like to see Manchester play.'

Pre-test discussion with this group might have included the children identifying words within words, for example: man, an, chest, Chester, ever, ton; perhaps they might have been asked too to place 'n' in front of 'ever' and work out the new word. Plastic letters are often a good idea for children experiencing some difficulties in learning spellings. Also, for their informal test, the *following* week, this group might be given a simple sentence containing the words within words, for example: 'I like the man; I can see a chest; I like Manchester.' Emphasis is thus on repetition of words learned so that success may be ensured.

Teachers may display words to be learned on the word charts described earlier, and, as was suggested, a regular, brief feature of each day might be games involving the identification and spelling of these words, and also related words, for example: mine, dine, wine, feline or clean, bean, each, eat. (Perhaps 4 or 5 minutes after playtime would be a good idea for such games.)

I have found it a good idea to give the children special books for their spelling tests, and provided that teachers establish rules about the informal testing procedure which are recalled regularly, there is seldom any difficulty in administering three brief tests consecutively. It is suggested that the children not being tested undertake a 'quiet' activity while a group is being tested (though I have often found that children prefer to listen to the tests of others, and may attempt other groups' spellings on scrap paper). Tests generally take between 4 and 6 minutes each to administer; Friday seems a logical day for testing words learned during the week. Children within the same group may mark each other's tests, though teachers may like to check some of the work of the below average group. At the end of the tests, teachers may ask questions such as 'Who feels very pleased with their work?' or 'Does anyone want me to help them with their next test?' Like Schonell (1942), I urge teachers to ensure that all groups have had frequent, yet brief, instruction during the week to help them to be successful in their tests. After all, the aim is to promote the children's interest in spelling and to help them to succeed in spelling so that they can write many of the high-frequency words easily before leaving the infant school. As Burt (1947) stated, the type of spelling capacity that is required for practical purposes is the ability to spell words automatically.

Spelling instruction and teachers' vocabulary

As was noted in Chapter 6, it is important that teachers help pupils to understand the technical terms and concepts used in spelling (and reading). Terms which may confuse children include:

- letters (capital and small);

- words;

- sentences and lines of text (and the difference between them);

- full-stops (and their function, which is *not* to allow the reader to take a breath!);

- vowels (and the difference between long vowels as in 'hate' and short vowels as in 'hat');

- consonants (and the difference between 'hard' consonants, such as 'go', and 'soft' consonants, such as 'orange');

- question marks (and their function);

- 'look at the word carefully' (for some children the word 'careful' needs explicit clarification).

Children may be introduced gradually to these terms with frequent revision of their meaning. Moreover, I suggest that children be asked to show their understanding of the terms by trying to explain their understanding orally. Children's nods, smiles and choruses of 'yes' when we simply ask if they understand, may be masking partial or non-comprehension on the part of some children, particularly those experiencing some difficulties in learning to spell (and perhaps to read) (Mudd, 1987).

Writing materials

Todd (1982) and Botham (1990) refer to the fact that young children in particular may be stimulated to want to write if they are provided with attractive writing materials in the form of coloured writing implements and writing paper; Botham suggests pastel colours for the latter. However, some teachers may be afraid that the overuse of felt pens, for example, may be detrimental to children's letter formation. Smith (1977, p. 46) suggests that when young children are enjoying pattern making and learning to form letters, the use of a thick, soft lead pencil should be the main writing tool, although brush, crayon, chalk, felt pen, etc., will also be suitable and provide varied experience. Interestingly, though, Sassoon (1990, p. 37) states that: '. . . many young children dislike the fat pencils that have been supplied to infant schools for many years'. It seems that teachers need to consider and plan handwriting materials very carefully – in addition to planning handwriting styles, etc.

Botham goes on to suggest that teachers of reception children may try putting writing areas alongside a wall (or walls) instead of having four tables together where the children are all facing each other. The main advantage of putting tables alongside walls is that the children are able to concentrate more easily since there is generally less distraction for them. She recommends pale blue/green backing paper on the wall to reflect a peaceful atmosphere.

Copying texts

As has been stated previously, 'blind' copying of spelling does not necessarily promote the learning of spellings; and certainly during the past two decades at least, copying work from blackboards has been generally denigrated since it is considered to be teacher-centred learning. Conversely, the last two decades have evidenced an increasing number of junior children copying large chunks of text from books related to topic work.

Yet, it has been found that in many cases the children do not understand what they are copying – such work is often justified on the grounds that it has been selected by the child. While considering that this type of copying has little value (apart from keeping the child occupied) I suggest that infant (and junior) children may benefit from a certain amount of 'thoughtful' copying; the work to be copied having been discussed by the teacher and children and understood by the latter. It may be undertaken as part of the children's handwriting instruction, and may include:

- poems or rhymes (or parts of them) chosen by teachers and/or children;

- proverbs;

- extracts from favourite books;

- jokes (including puns);

- songs to be sung in school concerts;

- words of 'pop' songs;

- brief notices, for example, information about a school trip or a 'bring and buy' sale. (This is definitely real writing used for a real purpose.)

Of course, teachers will find other examples of writing which children may copy while, at the same time, practising their handwriting skills. Thoughtful copying (after teacher/child discussion) provides a writing model in which children may observe how adult writers use language, rhythm, rhyme, alliteration, punctuation, etc., to help to communicate their 'message' (and, of course, children may be encouraged to use a modification of the Look/Cover – Write/Check method of transferring the message to paper). Moreover, even young children may begin to build up their own anthologies of poems and rhymes and, if they wish, they may read their favourites to other members of the class, thereby giving tangible status to literacy. The more that young children are able to see, read, discuss and copy examples of a variety of writing models, the more likely they are to develop their own writing for a variety of writing purposes.

Summary of suggestions for early spelling instruction

It is suggested that by the *end* of the infant school, children should have knowledge about a fairly wide area of spelling (and reading) related skills which may include:

The alphabet

Children should know names of letters and sounds of letters, and have developed an awareness of the relationship between sound and symbol, and also a gradual awareness that they cannot rely only on auditory analysis since letter sounds do not always have a constant representation in writing. Children should also know the sequences of the letters of the alphabet so that they are able to use dictionaries, etc., effectively.

At this point, I think it would be helpful if I remind readers that, as was noted in Chapter 3, there are 44 sounds (that is phonemes) in the most well-known English accent (received pronunciation) and also give Joyce Morris' groupings for these 44 phonemes (see page 134). I find Morris' (1984) suggestions for grouping the 44 phonemes very useful.

Vowels

Children should be helped to differentiate the different vowel sounds (and these are sometimes confused by children in the early stages of reading/writing). Also, children should be aware of 'long' and 'short' vowel sounds referred to earlier, and vowels embedded in names of the alphabet (for example, R/ar; L/el in words such as car/tar, tell/well). The frequent function of the letter 'y' as a vowel may also be discussed, as in 'happy' or 'very'.

Common consonant digraphs

For example, ch-sh-th-ph.

Common vowel digraphs

For example, oo-ee-ou-ai-ea. Some year 2 children may be made aware gradually that some of these digraphs have different sounds (good/food/; out/pour; each/great; said/paid). Since, in spelling instructions, stress is on the visual aspects of print as well as the auditory aspects, these words may be grouped together when discussing word families.

44 phonemes with their major spelling patterns (the numbers are for reference purposes only)

20 vowel sounds	*24 consonant sounds*	*Some other consonant patterns*

'short' vowel sounds

20 vowel sounds	*24 consonant sounds*	*Some other consonant patterns*
1 **a**pple	1 **b**at	double consonants: ff, ck
2 **e**gg	2 **c**at (**k**it)	clusters (initial): sk, sp, st, cl, cr
3 **i**nk	3 **d**in	scr, str
4 **o**range	4 **f**ish	clusters (end): sk, sp, st, ps, nds,
5 **u**mbrella	5 **g**o	nks
6 p**o**tato (this has an indistinct vowel sound or *schwa*)	6 **h**ave	silent letters: **k**nit, thum**b**
	7 **j**ump	
	8 **l**et	
Long vowel sounds	9 **m**an	
7 **a**pe p**ai**n s**ay**	10 **n**et	
8 **e**ve p**ee**l s**ea**l	11 **p**at	
9 **i**ce l**ie** h**igh**	12 **r**un	
10 m**o**de s**oa**k t**oe**	13 **s**et	
11 fl**u**te p**oo**l	14 **t**ap	
12 h**oo**k	15 **v**iolin	
	16 **w**ant	
Other vowel sounds	17 **y**et	
13 ball w**a**lk s**aw**	18 **z**oo	
14 st**ar**	(hou**s**es)	
15 b**ir**d h**er**mit	19 **sh**op	
16 m**ou**th cl**ow**n	20 **ch**in	
17 c**oi**l b**oy**	21 **th**e	
18 sq**uare** ch**air**	22 **th**ing	
19 **ear** d**eer** h**ere**	23 si**ng**	
20 g**our**d p**oor** c**ure**	24 televi**si**on	

NB 'q' and 'x' are redundant as 'basic' phonemes.

(Adapted from Morris (1984)).

Common blends of consonants and vowels

For example, at-ay-ew-it.

Common word endings (suffixes)

For example, ing-al-ed-er-es.

High-frequency words

It is recommended that by the *end* of year 2, children should be able to write between 30 and 100 high-frequency words 'automatically'. Naturally, the order in which spelling related skills are introduced will vary according to pupils' needs and their relation to work in the classroom. Clearly, too, different schools will set different goals for children to reach by the end of year 2; what is important is that there should be goals, and these should be plainly defined.

Whatever goals are set by teachers, spelling instruction should combine drawing children's attention to the visual and auditory aspects of print, with increasing emphasis on the former. Also, attention should be given to memory recall together with developing the children's articulatory abilities. Motor control may be promoted and improved via pattern-making, which leads on to correctly formed letters (whether joined, unjoined or accompanied by 'exit' strokes).

Above all, instruction should aim to stimulate children's interest in the writing process and to promote confidence in their own abilities.

In all the preceding suggestions for promoting children's understanding of the writing process, teacher/child discussion has played a vital part since, as Jerry Zutell (1980) stated:

> The development of spelling proficiency seems to involve both cognitive and linguistic processes, as such it requires the active, exploring participation of the learner. (p. 64)

I would add to this the fact that active exploration needs to be led by teachers who can inspire active exploration and thought on the part of the learner. The need for discussion (among children as well as among teachers and children) is further emphasised by Barnes and Todd (1977) who observe that teaching without exploratory talk expects pupils to arrive without having travelled.

In Chapter 3 we saw that Schonell (1942 and 1957) advocated systematic and brief, but regular, periods of spelling instruction accompanied by regular testing in order to let both teachers and children mark progress and/or difficulties. Despite his many critics who generally refer to the pointlessness of spelling lists compiled by teachers, there is still much to recommend his ideas regarding systematic and regular spelling instruction, particularly if related (as we have seen it may be) to children's work and to work in the classroom. After all, skills such as swimming, playing the piano or driving a car all require regular, systematic instruction and practice if the skill is to be acquired effectively; and the earlier that any skill is practised, the easier it is to learn.

Informal group tests (related to children's abilities) which may be marked by the children, give status to spelling and confidence to the children as they become aware of their progress in spelling (and writing). If, however, some children are not making progress, then such regular, informal tests will highlight any difficulties at an early stage. Thus, remedial instruction may be given long before the children move to the junior school where, because of their difficulties, they may become introverted or trouble-makers and, later, even semi-literate adults, who often spend years of misery in trying to hide their problems from society and sometimes even from their families. The need for remedial help may also be detected if teachers construct some form of screening tests at the beginning of year 2, so that more specific difficulties may be detected and given appropriate attention. (Some methods for helping children with severe spelling difficulties will be discussed in Chapter 9.)

The main aim of the spelling instruction referred to in this chapter is to help children to become responsible for their own learning in a gradual manner; once children are able to accept this responsibility, they are generally well on the way to becoming effective spellers and writers, who have been encouraged, as the National Curriculum suggests, to develop from invented spelling towards conventional accuracy.

Conclusion

As was stated in Chapter 1, the National Curriculum has provided the basis and opportunity for a uniform description of the attainment and progress of pupils through all stages of school; and this has included spelling. Yet, though its statements of attainment and programmes of study provide descriptions of *what* children should know at different stages, they do not clarify *how* teachers may help children to achieve these attainment targets. I have tried to remedy the National Curriculum's lack of explicitness with respect to methodology by putting forward my suggestions for instructing young children in writing and spelling. It is possible that my tone has, at times, seemed over-directive. However, I should like to restate the fact that my suggestions are merely a starting point which will, I hope, provoke teachers and potential teachers into thinking carefully about their own instructional methods for improving children's writing and spelling, and discussing their thoughts with other members of staff or other potential teachers.

It is surely in the early stages that children acquire (or do not acquire) good habits; habits which may form a solid base of knowledge about the writing process which will enable them to progress through school with confidence and wanting to move on to spelling knowledge and writing of a more sophisticated nature.

8 Effective teaching of spelling – Key Stage 2

This chapter aims to provide continuity from the previous chapter in which it was suggested that, as children leave the top class in the infant school, they should have acquired correct letter-formation skills and knowledge regarding the sound/symbol correspondence of print. They should be aware that the letters of our alphabet may represent more than one sound and also be aware of common letter sequences and the probabilities of these occurring. They should be able to spell quite a large number of high-frequency words (which are often irregular in terms of sound/symbol correspondence).

Bennett *et al.* (1984, p. 128) found that in many schools, requisitions for spellings constituted the predominant teacher/pupil exchange in many lessons. Hopefully, if the children arriving in the junior school from the infant school have been encouraged to establish positive attitudes towards spelling, and to begin to be responsible for their own learning, then requisitions for spellings and spelling 'queues' will cease to dominate so many lessons. Unless children have been shown to have difficulties related to the auditory aspects of language (and these will be discussed in the chapter on children with spelling difficulties) the junior child is generally at the stage for concentrating more attention on the visual aspects of print. There should be no teachers' suggestions to 'sound it out' if a child evidences difficulties in spelling a word, since 'sounding out' usually only works effectively if one knows the spelling alternatives to be selected for particular words; for example, the good speller knows that 'once' may *not* be sounded out to produce the correct spelling, whereas he or she knows that 'went' may be successfully sounded out.

The junior child's independent control of his or her learning needs to be promoted even further, and this includes helping some children to become skilful in looking carefully at words to detect parts which may be difficult for them, and in helping them to check spellings for accuracy by the independent, effective use of resources. For some children, the avoidance of 'blind' copying needs to be reinforced. Children's vocabularies will be extending, and there should be a greater selectiveness regarding the type of words required for various writing situations and audiences. The National Curriculum (Attainment Target 3: writing, level 4) suggests that pupils should be able to 'write, in addition to stories, instructions, accounts or explanations, perhaps of a scientific investigation' and 'present information and express feelings in forms such as letters, poems, invitations, posters, etc.' All these writing activities require quality of content plus correctness in terms of spelling, grammar, punctuation and handwriting since they are generally intended for an audience which extends beyond themselves and their teacher.

Junior children's interest in our language may be promoted if they are given information about the origins of our language and the influence of other languages upon English (which may include the use of etymological dictionaries). Of course, such information is dependent on the teacher's knowledge about our language. We see then, that in the junior school, children's spelling strategies are refined and targets of learning related to written language are greatly extended. It is, however, recommended that teachers of first year juniors should ease them gradually into their new learning by brief but regular revision of knowledge related to spelling and writing. This is essential for promoting confidence within children and in bridging the gap between infant and junior school, and also for helping any new children to understand and 'catch up with' the school's methods of spelling and writing instruction. As before, it is suggested that much of the instruction be given to the class or to groups, as well as to children who require individual attention. As in the previous chapter, stress will be on methodology rather than on word lists; also, spelling instruction will be considered mainly as it relates to the children's written work.

Children's writing

It is suggested that before any writing is undertaken, there should be ample and explicit teacher/child discussion regarding the nature of the writing required; writing tasks may be clarified if the teacher provides models of the type of writing required (which may be in the form of a letter, poem, poster, etc.). Spellings which are likely to be central to the writing, and perhaps arising from teacher/child discussions, may be written on the board or in some more permanent form, such as wall-charts or word banks (these were referred to in the previous chapter). If words can be grouped in 'families' according to their visual structure, then it is often helpful in reinforcing the children's visual recall of the words. In order to illustrate some of the points made, and also to show how writing and spelling instruction may be integrated, I intend to describe a lesson taken by me recently with a class of children aged between 7 and 9 years. (I was not the class teacher, though I had worked with the children on several previous occasions.) The lesson given was modelled partially on advice given by Donald Graves (1983) to teachers hoping to improve children's writing skills. (See Chapter 3 of this book.) The lesson was also based on the author's experiences of extending children's writing.

Graves' methods were considered somewhat formal in the 1980s when child-centred and less-structured teaching was generally in vogue. Interestingly, though, his recommendations to teachers combine traditional methods with methods which cater, too, for individual needs. For example, he suggests that teachers address classes as a whole while discussing and/or planning *their* own writing with the children. Also Graves' writing 'rules' regarding quietness and lack of movement may be regarded as very formal, yet his recommendations for teachers working individually, in 'conference' with about six children per lesson (and at least four writing lessons per week), mean that individual progress and difficulties can be monitored. Moreover, Graves suggests that teachers do not consider firstly the mechanics of the writing process (for example, spelling, handwriting, punctuation, grammar), but that they consider what the child has written about, and this involves encouraging the child to speak freely about his or her work via the teacher's open-ended questions.

'The teacher attends to what children know and helps them to speak about their topics' (Graves, 1983, p. 104). This certainly does not mean that Graves ignores the mechanics of writing. Indeed, section III of his book (entitled 'Help Children Learn the Skills They Need') is devoted to improving not only what children write, but also how they write it. Regular recording of each child's development and discussing both progress and difficulties with the child is also an essential part of Graves' philosophy.

The more recent DES report by Robin Alexander *et al.* (1992) similarly stresses the need for teachers to demonstrate practical activities, to pose different kinds of questions, and to help pupils understand how well they have done (p. 31). They conclude, too, that teachers need the skills and judgement to be able to select and apply whichever organisational strategy – class, group and individual – is appropriate to the task in hand (p. 30).

Since the children were soon to move into the 'top' class, it seemed a relevant time to think about their first class in school, indeed, their first day at school. The ultimate writing goal, therefore, was to express their feelings (whether positive or negative) on their first day in school. The writing could be in either prose or poetry. Thus, on our first meeting, I read Roger McGough's poem to them, 'First Day at School' (1983); the children had copies of the poem. They were then given a few minutes to read the poem for themselves and discuss it with a partner. A class discussion followed on McGough's main feelings of confusion which were emphasised by his use of question marks. For example,

> Waiting for the bell to go. (To go where?)
>
> All round, the railings.
>
> Are they to keep out wolves and monsters?

Following this, we discussed our recollections of our first days at school. On a second meeting with the class, some of the main observations made on our first meeting were recalled, followed by a re-reading of McGough's poem. Having then suggested that the children might recall in prose or poetry their first day at school, the class was invited to suggest words or phrases that might be useful in their writing. These words were written down as they were suggested, that is, in no special order, and down one side of the board. Later, with the children's help, I placed these in various 'families' as illustrated below:

playground	McGough	arrived	
sound	(van Gogh)	frightened	a *mixture* of verbs,
found	rough	puzzled	but all in the
water-fountain	cough	scared	past tense
	thought	excited	
	although		

nervous, computer, photocopier
plasticine-plastic (the latter was a word introduced by me to show the relationship of the two words)

In the list headed by 'McGough', the words 'rough' and 'cough' had been included simply because the children related them to the pattern of 'McGough'; they were not required for their written work. Similarly, 'van Gogh' was added to the list at the children's request because they had previously done a project on van Gogh. Though the latter's name is not visually identical to the others in the list, it seemed a good idea to illustrate options in different spelling systems.

Before the actual writing began, I gave the children a few minutes to write any words they thought they would need (or that interested them) in their personal dictionaries using the Look/Cover – Write/Check method (see page 40). After 'personal' words had been written, we revised our rules for the writing session. These were simply that the writing was to be done in silence for the first 15 minutes, with me also writing about my first day at school; it was stressed that no children were to ask me or any other child for help with spellings. As in the previous chapter, children who could not spell a word were recommended to write either the first and last letters of difficult spellings, or to try the word for themselves. When children use the latter method, they often relate what they can hear to what they write down, with more able spellers also using their knowledge of probable letter combinations (as suggested by Peters (1985)). Thus, 'work' might logically be written as 'werk' since the 'er' combination is common. However, the child who writes it as 'wuk' is clearly paying attention *only* to what is heard, and not to any recalled letter patterns. This is why I do not favour (as Peters does), the rubbing out of spelling miscues as children write in the correct version; I consider that original miscues (if neatly crossed out with the correct version written above) may be valuable in helping to detect children with potentially severe spelling difficulties (they also help children to note their own progress).

During the writing and thinking period of 15 minutes, the children naturally varied greatly with respect to the amount written. It is vital to ensure that children do not measure their success by the quantity they write and to reassure any children who are not able to put their thoughts easily into words that not everyone finds the writing task easy. In fact, though, I find that an initial period of quietness, during which the children see the teacher writing too, helps the children to concentrate their thoughts and, usually, most (if not all) children produce work which is of a higher standard than that produced during periods in which there is constant movement, borrowings (of rulers, pencils, etc.), and oral interruptions by the teacher and by children. Naturally, it may take some time for this type of work to become a matter of routine, and children need regular reminders about any rules made, and why they should be observed. Moreover, some teachers find such ideas alien to their normal teaching methods. I would suggest to these teachers that they try out a few silent writing periods, and bear in mind that most professional writers ensure that there are no interruptions while they 'compose' their work. (I do know some writers who work better to a background accompaniment of music, but such music cannot really be classified as 'interruptions'.)

After 15 minutes, I stopped my writing and informed the children that I

142

would be moving round the group to give any help required (the tables were placed so that six children were grouped together). I reminded the children that they were not to come to me with their questions, and suggested that they check over their writing when it was finished and then continue with some personal reading. Checking included re-reading for meaning and checking the accuracy of spellings and punctuation. Correction of misspellings could include the use of class and personal dictionaries, and words displayed on the board (the class did not have word banks). The children were reminded to use the Look/Cover – Write/Check method of correcting errors, and to enter corrected spellings into personal dictionaries as well as their written work.

As I moved from group to group, I dealt with their various queries, some of which related to their use of question marks, speech marks and also their choice of vocabulary. If spellings were required, I wrote them in the margin of the child's work near to where the spelling was required with the child watching me write the word and listening to me saying aloud the whole word and the letter names as I did so; this may encourage children to do the same and thereby reinforce their learning. If the child had attempted the spelling for him or herself (incorrectly), I underlined the 'tricky' part of the word (with the child watching). For example, if the child wrote 'fech' for 'fetch', I underlined the letter 't' in the correct version. The children were encouraged to use the Look/Cover – Write/Check method to transfer any corrected words to their work – after first crossing out the incorrect spelling neatly. They were further encouraged to enter the word in their personal dictionaries (still using the Look/Cover – Write/Check method).

Like Graves (1983) and Peters (1985), I do not consider that there is time to give spelling instruction during writing lessons. However, I did make a note of any common difficulties and also any individual difficulties (together, of course, with the individual's name). Also, I collected in the children's personal dictionaries when I collected in their work for marking so that I could check that their entries were correct and make a note of any recurring entries.

About 5 minutes before the 'official' end of the lesson, the children were asked to stop writing or reading and to read over their work with a partner with a view to sharing its contents with the class. There were more volunteers than we had time for, but we did manage to hear the experiences of three children during their first day at school. These three were selected to represent varying levels of ability. (There is a temptation to listen only to the 'good' children.) The class was informed that there would be time to hear more of their experiences the next day (including mine, if they wished!). In this way, emphasis was given (and quite rightly) to the content of the children's work. The whole of the second lesson lasted 1 hour and 10 minutes.

Marking their written work

In order that my initial concentration remained on the content of the work, I read through to the end of each piece of work, and then made my written comment/reaction regarding their recalled experiences. Comments on structure, vocabulary, punctuation, spelling, etc., followed my comments on the work's content. Since I was not the class teacher, I was not able to comment upon any progress (or otherwise) in these areas, and so I made written remarks concerning the general content of their work, noting areas of difficulty. Like Peters, I did not correct all the children's spelling or punctuation errors, I concentrated on the more important ones. However, children whose work is to be displayed or used in some other 'public' way should, after year 2, be fully corrected; they generally understand the reasons for such correctness and like to know that their work will be presented in the best possible way. I have included two examples of their marked draft work in order to demonstrate my marking (and remarking) methods. It is probable that some teachers will disagree with some of my suggestions; this is as it should be since I merely aim to stimulate teachers' thinking about their own marking systems.

Rachel (figure 8.1) had not allowed herself a margin, so I had to write spelling and grammatical corrections below my remarks about her content. Since her spelling errors were few, I have referred to them all ('couldn't', 'didn't', etc., proved to have been written incorrectly by several of the children and so they were discussed with the whole class the next day).

As stated in my comment on his work, (see 8.2a) I found Steven's use of repetition effective; it added continuity to his main idea in the poem. His use of punctuation had been based on McGough's punctuation in his poem. (An example of a child using another person's work as a writing model.) Steven's notes above his work indicate that he had spent some time in getting his ideas together. He decided later to copy out his original work for display (see figure 8.2b).

On the following day (our third meeting), before handing back their written work, I asked the children to recall some of the words containing

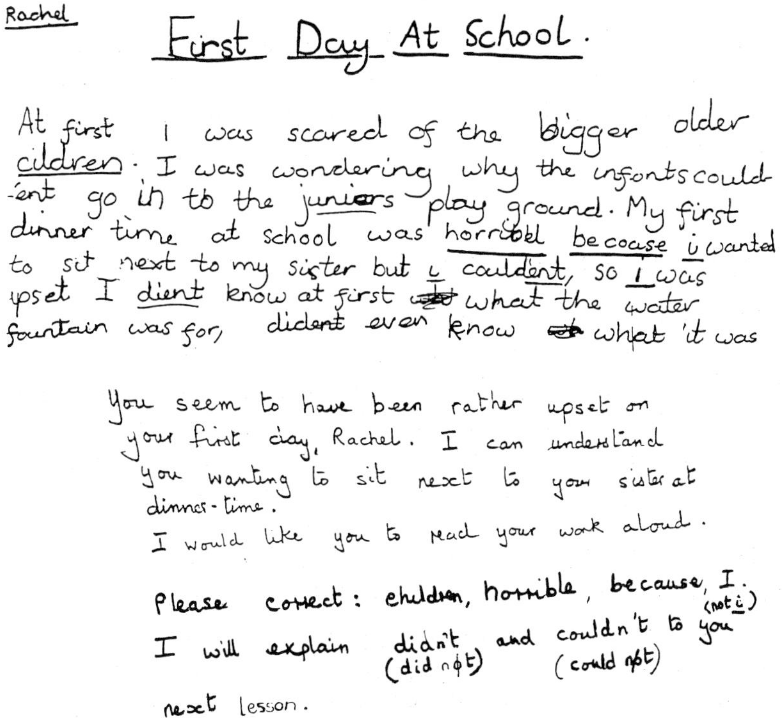

Rachel

First Day At School.

At first I was scared of the bigger older cildren. I was wondering why the infonts could-ent go in to the juniors play ground. My first dinner time at school was horribbl becoase i wanted to sit next to my sister but i couldent, so I was upset I dient know at first what the water fountain was for, dident even know what it was

You seem to have been rather upset on your first day, Rachel. I can understand you wanting to sit next to your sister at dinner-time.
I would like you to read your work aloud.

Please correct: children, horrible, because, I.
(not i)
I will explain didn't and couldn't to you
(did not) (could not)

next lesson.

Figure 8.1 Rachel describes her first day at school

the 'ough' letter string; as they recalled them, I wrote them on the board, saying the letter names as I wrote. The children were then asked to put the words into sentences to consolidate their learning. We also discussed briefly the use of the apostrophe of omission in words, such as 'didn't', 'couldn't', by writing 'did not', 'could not'. This class revision of spellings and grammar took only about 8 minutes. (Had I been their class teacher, I could have moved on to their selections for group learning to be used in dictated sentences at the end of the week. Group dictations will be discussed later in this chapter.)

The written work was then handed out and children who wished to do so were invited to read their work to the rest of the class. Some children whose work was particularly interesting or who needed a 'confidence boost' were requested to read their work aloud via my written comments, though no child was forced to do so. One girl asked me to read her work for her. At the end of the class readings, the children asked me to read my school experience which was in narrative form; I must say that I was impressed by some children, like Steven, who had managed to present

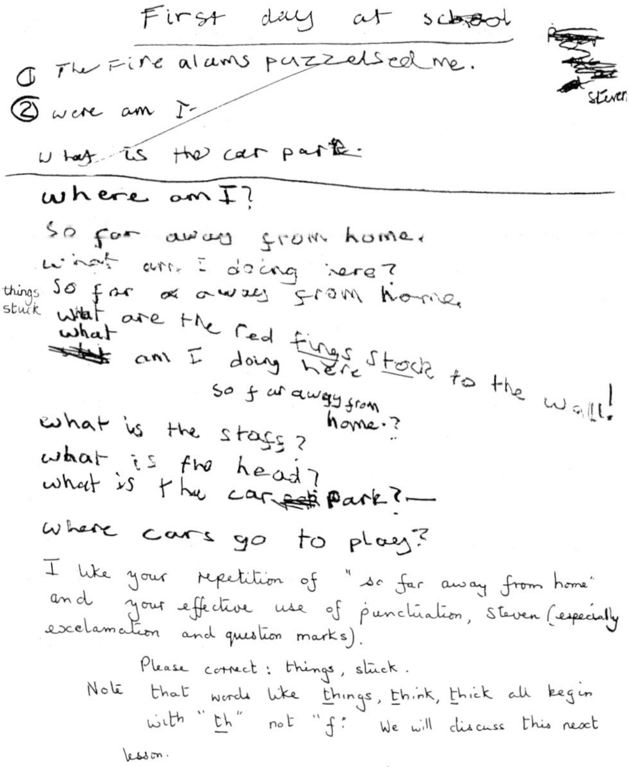

First day at school

① The fire alarm puzzelsed me.
② were am I-
what is the car park.

_____

where am I?
So far away from home.
what am I doing here?
things So far away from home.
stuck what are the red things stuck to the wall!
what
~~what~~ am I doing here
So far away from
home."
what is the staff?
what is the head?
what is the car ~~pak~~ park?—
where cars go to play?

I like your repetition of "so far away from home"
and your effective use of punctuation, Steven (especially
exclamation and question marks).

Please correct: things, stuck.
Note that words like things, think, thick all begin
with "th" not "f". We will discuss this next
lesson.

Figure 8.2a Steven's poem reflects some of Roger McGough's style

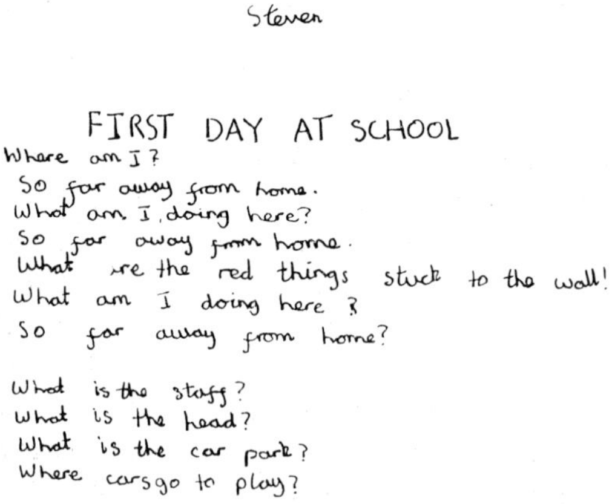

Steven

FIRST DAY AT SCHOOL
Where am I?
So far away from home.
What am I doing here?
So far away from home.
What are the red things stuck to the wall!
What am I doing here?
So far away from home?

What is the staff?
What is the head?
What is the car park?
Where cars go to play?

Figure 8.2b Steven's 'refined' copy of his poem

their *first* drafts in the form of a poem. (Oral readings took about 20 minutes.)

The following 5 minutes were devoted to the children placing any corrections above their incorrect (crossed out) words and entering them into their personal dictionaries from memory; once this was done, the children were encouraged to carry on with some personal reading. After the 5 minutes of correction time, the children were given a further 20 minutes in which they could either copy out their written work for display in the classroom, or they could copy out McGough's poem (perhaps with a view to including it in their personal anthology books). Obviously, the Look/Cover – Write/Check method is not applicable in the case of a poem (or long text), but children who made this choice were asked to pay careful attention to any spellings they considered 'tricky' and also the punctuation, especially McGough's use of question marks. A third option was to continue with some personal reading. During this time, I moved around the groups, helping children with their queries. Several children had included their own direct speech or that of a member of their family in their writing, but were generally unsure of the correct use of inverted commas to signify direct speech. Thus, I was able to instruct this group of children in the use of 'speech marks'.

At the end of this lesson, the children were delighted to be asked by the teacher of year 6 children to read some of their work to her class the following day. During the next playtimes and lunchtime, the children were heard practising the oral readings of their writing; those who had opted to write out McGough's poem worked, with my help, on a 'choral' reading of the poem. Since the top juniors were leaving at the end of the week, recollections of first days at school seemed relevant both in retrospect and prospect. (The third lesson lasted just over an hour.)

Before moving on to the next section of this chapter, I should like to make three general observations relevant to the lesson just taken. Firstly, it is essential that children are seated so that they can see the board as the teacher writes and discusses writing and spellings. In many schools, children are no longer seated in rows, and unless teachers ensure that all the children are facing the board, many will have a distorted view of the teacher's writing; and since the emphasis is mainly on the visual aspects of writing, it is essential that the children see clearly what is being written. It is equally important to ensure that the children are able to see the teacher's face in order to help them to hear clearly. Our partial dependence on lip-reading (albeit unconscious) when we are listening to someone speak often becomes evident if the speaker turns away from us as they are talking; also we often have to 'strain' our ears as we listen to tape-recordings of people speaking.

Secondly, with respect to the Look/Cover – Write/Check method of encouraging children to learn spellings, I should like to include my own amendments to the method. I encourage children to say aloud the complete word as they first look at it and before looking *carefully* at it; in my opinion, this helps to emphasise the 'whole' along with the 'parts'. Moreover, teachers should be aware that looking at a word carefully and paying attention to the details in it is by no means easy for some children (though, admittedly, some are able to recall details of words seen with very little obvious difficulty). In fact, some children (and adult novice writers) assume that merely looking briefly at a word will help it to become imprinted in their memory. Thus, teachers need to illustrate effective looking by means of many practical examples, so that if the word 'enough' is being looked at carefully, the child may note the 'en' beginning of the word and the fairly common 'ough' pattern. As in the lesson described, other 'ough' words, such as 'rough', 'tough', 'cough', 'though', may also be considered in order to reinforce that particular letter string. Also, children may need training in identifying which parts of spelling may be difficult for them, although children who have severe difficulties in learning spellings sometimes spell the same word differently on different occasions. (This will be given more attention in the chapter on children with spelling difficulties.)

Thirdly, the teachers' handwriting should reflect the style advocated by the school, and this should apply to their writing in the children's books and on the board. Children learn by example and should see teachers providing models upon which to base their writing. (I must admit that my personal writing for *myself* is somewhat untidy, but I always try to improve and adapt my style when writing for children.) College students on teaching practice do not always seem aware of this, and some of them provide rather 'scrappy' models of handwriting, and even spelling and grammar when writing on boards and in children's books.

In order to help children to understand for themselves the value of well-presented work (in terms of spelling, handwriting, etc.) which also has merit in terms of content, it may be useful from time to time to let the children evaluate two pieces of writing specially prepared by the teacher for the class of children. It is suggested that one piece (1) of writing is 'correct' in terms of handwriting, spelling and punctuation, but fairly uninspiring in terms of content. The second piece (2) may leave much to be desired with respect to the secretarial aspects of writing, but may be far more interesting in terms of content. For example:

1   I went to the park and bought an ice-cream. Then I saw my friend and he bought me one too. We had a nice time and then went home and watched TV.

2   As I wook up i was very ecsited becoz my mum and dad sed I cold go with my frend to see the red arows give a demo of arobaticks Peter calld for me and we sortid are pakt lunchis out crisps pop and delishus pechis the demo was brilant.

Before the children see the written texts (perhaps on an overhead projector) it is suggested that the teacher reads the texts aloud so that the children's first judgement is on the content of the work. Then the children may be allowed to see the two pieces of writing, and after several minutes of discussion time (perhaps in twos) teachers may invite general comments from the class regarding content and presentation. I have found that when children (and college students) evaluate other people's work, they are usually much more critical of errors than teachers. At the end of the discussion period, teachers may point out that most people are influenced greatly by presentation and correctness when they first look at a piece of written work. The 'moral' of the lesson is that handwriting and spelling do matter, though content should be their major concern. Thus, children's aims should be to present *final* drafts of written work which evidence well-presented, qualitative writing. However, as Graves (1983) suggested, not all children's work is worth re-writing, and children should be involved in decisions regarding re-drafting. Of course, children need to understand, too, that first drafts and notes are really only for the benefit of the author and may be accompanied by many crossings out since they reflect thinking, re-thinking and getting down ideas while the thoughts are 'flowing'. If we do not make this clear, then some children may become obsessed by treating their first drafts as final copies, perhaps at the expense of quality writing.

Reference has been made to children's use of spelling resources in the class lesson described previously. It is thus intended to discuss some resources which teachers may wish to provide for children; and, more importantly, to discuss how teachers may ensure that children are not only using them, but using them effectively.

Effective use of class dictionaries

In most junior classes there is usually a wide selection of dictionaries, with some children having a dictionary each. However, though children are continually urged by adults to 'Use your dictionary if you don't know a spelling', there is frequently little time given to training children in the effective and speedy use of dictionaries. It is not uncommon to see children (and adults) trying frustratedly to locate a word by (apparently) skimming through all the words beginning with 'i' or even 'e' as they try to find the word 'imagine'. Effective dictionary skills cannot be learned in one 30-minute lesson, and yet we hear teachers commenting, 'But I taught them how to use their dictionaries at the beginning of the year.' Like most other aspects of the spelling process, for some children, effective and speedy dictionary skills need frequent (though brief) and explicit instruction. (Of course, other children, possibly used to handling dictionaries at home, may experience few difficulties in dictionary use.) It may be helpful to some teachers if I describe a dictionary 'game' (based upon ideas by Joyce Todd (1982) which I have used successfully with year 3 children. Ideally, each child should have his or her own fairly simple dictionary (I have found *The Weetabix Wonderwords Illustrated Oxford Dictionary* (1990), published by Oxford University Press, to be very attractive to children and easy to use.)

At the first stage, teachers should ensure that all the children know the alphabet sequence correctly and speedily, and that they are able to write it down from memory. (If it was learned thoroughly in the infant school, then there are generally few problems.) It is a good idea to let the children write out the alphabet at the back of their personal dictionaries, with the teacher checking for accuracy and supplying remedial help where necessary.

At the second stage, teachers may explain *why* dictionary skills are useful, and demonstrate how, for example, we use the first letter of a word to find its approximate location in the dictionary. Children and teacher may then find together some words beginning with letters near the beginning, the middle and the end of the alphabet (perhaps, b, m and w). At this stage, teachers should point out to the children that the dictionaries are being used mainly as spelling resources and not resources for obtaining the meanings of words – though children are often pleased to discover that they know (and can read) the meaning of a word. When stage three is reached, the children may be grouped in twos or fours around tables and given envelopes containing ten small cards, all with different letters of the alphabet written on them. The children should not take the cards out of the envelopes until directed to do so. (All groups should receive the same letters and teachers should keep a careful check on which letters are used.)

The children then take it in turns to pull out a card from the envelope and place it face upwards on the table; that child then says the name of the letter followed by the word 'Go'. The group then use their individual dictionaries to find a stated number of words (perhaps varying according to the ability of the group) starting with that letter; these words may then be written in their jotters – this is good training in visual recall if 'blind' copying is discouraged. (I make the additional proviso that the children should only write words in their jotters which they can read, and whose meanings they know.) This is repeated until all the letters have been used. If any groups forget the alphabetical sequence, they may use their personal dictionaries as a source of reference. As groups finish, they may indicate this to the teacher who can then tell them the amount of time they have taken for the game. Some of each group's words may be said aloud (and/ or discussed briefly) to conclude the game. It should be stressed that this is only a game whereby they may improve their individual efficiency and speed; it is not a game in which they try to compete with others. Once children are ready to do so (and this may not apply to the whole class), they move on to stage four.

At stage four, children may be given ten cards containing the first two letters of words to be found, perhaps with the second letter being found at, or near, the beginning of the alphabet, for example: ab, eb, ha, me. As before, it is vital that all progressive stages in dictionary use are clearly demonstrated by the teacher with the children actively involved in trying out similar stages.

At later stages, common, but sometimes rather difficult, letter blends and digraphs which occur at the beginning of words may be used with speed games, for example: wh, th, con, pre, qu, kn. Some children (often those who are interested in language and spelling) may enjoy trying to locate unusual spellings (or what Todd calls 'tricks'). For example, rhubarb, cycle, psalm, chemist, choir, though they will still generally need to be given some clues regarding the nature of such words' irregularities. It should be remembered, too, that children differ greatly in their ability to use dictionaries effectively, and some may take two or more years before they are able to locate words speedily. Indeed, there are some children who become so dependent upon spelling according to sound that they may make little progress in their dictionary skills, even by year 6.

David Moseley and Catherine Nicol have written *ACE (Aurally Coded English) Spelling Dictionary* (1986), published by LDA. It aims to help children who find spelling difficult, though it does require the user to understand the difference between long and short vowels and also to have the ability to isolate the first vowel sound in a word, and to recognise the number of syllables in a word. Therefore, the dictionary may *sound* rather daunting; however, several tutors in adult basic education have helped their students to use the dictionary quite effectively. The authors claim that the book helps students to 'Find words quickly and improve your spelling'; I think that spelling is only improved if teachers (or tutors) actively help students with spelling difficulties to find a method of learning spellings which suits them as individuals. I think teachers need to make up their own minds upon the book's usefulness (or otherwise).

Methods like the ones described earlier with groups of children may also be used to help children in their effective and speedy location of information in reference books (especially encyclopaedias). The success of such methods depends upon clear, regular, brief instruction in which the children are given ample opportunities to learn by active participation.

Etymological dictionaries

Etymological dictionaries (which give information relating to word origins) may be introduced to children in years 5 and 6 in school. The use of such dictionaries, however, depends on the teacher's interest in this subject; unfortunately, I have found that many adults (including many student teachers) have never used etymological dictionaries. This being the case, and at the risk of seeming to patronise some readers, I will explain briefly how one may discover the origins of words.

Firstly, it is vital to establish that one's dictionary does actually provide information regarding the origins of words; many dictionaries, and especially 'pocket' ones, include only word meanings. Having established that etymological information is given, one may look up a word like *salary*. It is the information given after the word's meaning has been explained which is relevant to the word's origins. Thus, after explanations regarding salary being a fixed payment made by an employer at regular intervals, etc., we usually find square brackets containing information about the word's derivation. For example: [M.E.f.A.F. salarie, O.F. salaire f.L. salarium orig. soldier's salt-money (sal salt)].

To those inexperienced in locating the etymology of words, this information may seem rather complex. In fact, it is quite simple once one understands the abbreviations, and all dictionaries explain their abbreviations and symbols in their introductions or prefaces (of course, some abbreviations differ slightly in different dictionaries). In the example just given, M.E. = Middle English (this is English used between 1100 and 1450, see also page 15); f. = from; A.F. = Anglo-French; O.F. = Old French; L. = Latin.

Thus, the reader is informed that the word was first used between the twelfth and fifteenth centuries, and has French and Latin origins. I think that the added information about 'salt-money' is interesting, and clarifies what we mean when we say someone is 'worth their salt' (though it is possible that some etymological dictionaries will not supply this latter information).

Another word which I find interesting is *denim*; most etymological dictionaries will inform us that, apart from being a hard-wearing cotton fabric used for overalls, jeans, etc., it originated from the words 'serge de Nim' (Nim refers to Nîmes in southern France).

Once children's interest in our language is stimulated, I find that some become fascinated by discovering the roots of the language they use. Of course, teachers need to pave the way for this interest by discovering for themselves some of the very intriguing words in our language. I have included some words whose meaning I find interesting in the section headed 'Did you know?' (page 163).

Children who have acquired some grammatical knowledge (years 5 and 6, perhaps) may also be interested in the letters which appear after words in most dictionaries; these letters denote the word's grammatical function. For example: n (noun); vt (verb transitive); vi (verb intransitive); a (adjective); adv (adverb) and so on. Children do *not* need to know all those parts of speech; it may be sufficient (especially with respect to in/transitive verbs) to know what the letters signify. Children are often amused to find sl (slang) or vul (vulgar) after certain words which they locate; it helps them to realise that they are not the first ones to have used 'doubtful' words!

Word banks

In the previous chapter, reference was made to infant children's use of word banks as spelling resources; refined versions of these may be used in junior classes with words classified alphabetically and/or under headings of any project work. Thus, for example, words arising from a project on air-travel may be filed under the 'A' section of the word bank and may include project-related words, such as airplane, airport, aeroplane, flight, travel. If teachers firstly display topic-related words on a board or large paper, they may be discussed as part of their spelling instruction and arranged in groups. So, *travel* might be grouped with traveller, travelled and travelling; *flight* may be associated with fly and its irregular past tense, flew; and *height* may be associated with weight. These words may then be entered into the 'A' section of word banks and some may be cross-referenced (according to the children's needs) under their own alphabetical category. Homophones may be entered in word banks in context; thus, 'flew' might be illustrated by the sentence 'The bird flew away' and 'flu' might be illustrated by the sentence, 'I was very ill when I had flu'.

As with infant word banks, they should be constructed from sturdy card (preferably covered with plastic), revised regularly, and ideally there should be separate banks available to small groups of children. For younger or less able spellers, teachers and parents may provide illustrations (drawn by hand or taken from magazines, etc.) to help the children to identify words which they require.

Some alternative aids to spelling

Mnemonics

The Look/Cover – Write/Check method of learning spellings has been referred to many times already, though it should be acknowledged that some children (and adults) find mnemonics useful as an aid to learning spellings – especially humorous ones which are not too involved. Unfortunately, sometimes rather complicated mnemonics are taught which students cannot remember! (Mnemonics are designed to aid the memory and have their roots in Latin and Greek; Mnemosyne was the Greek goddess of memory and mother of the Muses.)

The most successful mnemonics are usually those which have relevance for the learner. However, I have included some mnemonics collected from a variety of sources, which have proved successful with a variety of learners of all ages who have difficulties in spelling particular words.

> Pretty Betty
> I don't w**ant** an **ant** in my p**ant**s
> Have a **pie**ce of **pie**

I saw my **fri**end on **Fri**day
*This **bus** is **bus**y
*U and I b**ui**ld a house
*__Al__ w**al**ked and t**al**ked about ch**al**k and st**al**ks
*He **kn**ew when he **kn**elt on his **kn**ees he had a **kn**ife in his **kn**itted
  knickers
It's gr**ea**t to take a br**ea**k and eat st**ea**k
I can h**ear** with my **ear**s
She did not sp**oil** the t**oil**et by putting s**oil** into it
A witch drinks tea and drops her aitches (or 'h') (cf which)
W**hen** I saw the **hen**, I fell in the p**en**
I shall t**ake** my r**ake** and m**ake** a garden by the l**ake**
W**hat** a silly **hat** she has!
Their cat is with **the** dog in **the**ir garden
It was not n**ight** when they saw the s**ight**. It was br**ight** and l**ight**
He is sitting **on** a t**on** of m**on**ey
The b**ean**s were cl**ean** so I put them with some l**ean** m**ea**t
The **other** lady was his m**other**
Her n**ice** driving l**ice**nce is full of **ice**
He tr**ies** and tr**ies** but he cannot kill the fl**ies**
She made a **sign**al for me to **sign** the paper with my **sign**ature
They **bomb**arded us with **bomb**s and so we ran to the t**omb** for
  shelter.

Examples marked * have been taken from Joy Pollock's book, *Signposts
to Spelling* (1980). If possible, it is a good idea to let the children decide
which part of such sentences should be underlined.

It is interesting to note that some mnemonics may associate words of
irregular sound/symbol correspondence with those of regular sound/
symbol correspondence (pretty/Betty). The effective use of mnemonics
requires the learner's visual, auditory, cognitive (thinking) and recall
skills to interact together. Words with silent letters in the middle may
prove difficult for even quite good spellers. If possible, I teach such
words along with a related word in which the silent letter is pronounced.
For example, 'The bombs bombarded the men (or bombardiers)', 'The
librarian worked in the library', 'The lady gave the signal to sign the
paper', 'In autumn there is an autumnal chill in the air'. Sentences like these
may represent part of the children's chosen dictations when their spelling
knowledge is tested (and revised). Of course, teachers will recall some
mnemonics of their own and also construct more to suit their children's
needs.

It is also sometimes helpful to ask children to *mispronounce* spellings which cause difficulty according to sound/symbol correspondence. Thus, *Wednesday* may be pronounced as Wed nez day; *February* may be pronounced as Feb roo ary; *except* may be pronounced as ex sept, and so on. This phonetic recall of the word (albeit the incorrect pronunciation) does stress the *visual* aspect of the word.

Moreover, to this day, when I write certain 'irregular' words, I sub-vocalise the word parts as they sound. I wonder if any readers still use this method with certain words.

Homophones

Homophones are words which sound the same but have different meanings. (*Homo* is from the Greek word meaning 'same'; *phone* is also from a Greek word meaning 'sound'.) Children who confuse homophones are not really making spelling errors since homophones depend upon the context for their spelling. Thus, the child who writes 'pair' for 'pear' needs to be taught the correct spelling for the context used, and since both spellings are fairly common words (and the errors are common), teachers may wish to discuss them with a group of children. Sentences such as 'The girl eats the pear and the peach' may reinforce the meaning and the 'ea' digraph. Personally, I would not try to teach the children the spelling of 'pair' at the same time; in my opinion, it is best to concentrate on one new piece of learning at a time. Discussions about 'pair' would follow in a different learning session.

The homophones their/there and the near-homophones where/were frequently cause difficulties for some novice writers. No doubt teachers will have methods for helping children to use them correctly, but I feel it important to advise them against making up 'rules' like one I hear so often, that is, *where* and *there* contain the word 'here', so if the sentences refer to place, use 'where' or 'there'. This statement is at best a generalisation, and I have worked with many confused novice writers who write sentences such as, 'There mother is in hospital'; or 'We where in the park.' These writers have assumed that they were correct since both sentences contained references to a place.

Usually, I do not teach the function of 'there' and 'where', instead I concentrate on the possessive pronoun 'their' and the verb 'were' (though it is not essential for children to know the grammatical names in order to understand the words' functions in sentences). When considering the word 'their', I relate it to other possessive pronouns: my, your, his, her, its, our, your, their. We then consider the use of these pronouns in similar sentences: I saw my dog; I saw his dog; I saw your dog; I saw our dog; I saw their dog. By substituting any one of these pronouns, children may check if they have used the correct 'their' homophone. For example, we could substitute 'his' for 'their' in the following sentence: 'They put their (his) books on the table'. The sentence still makes sense, although the meaning has changed slightly. Note that in the sentence, 'I put the books there', 'his' could not be substituted for 'there'. Similarly, I relate *were* to other phrases containing the past tense of the verb 'to be': I was out; You were out; He was out; She was out; It was out; We were out; You were out; They were out. Novice writers may check for accuracy by substituting 'were' for 'was'; if the sentence still makes sense (albeit ungrammatical) then the correct homophone has been used. For example: 'We were (was) on the bus'; but we could not substitute 'was' in the sentence, 'I don't know where (was) it is'.

Again, please note that it is not necessary for the learner to know the technical (grammatical) terms in order to differentiate homophones, though if the teacher is confident in using grammatical terms and explaining them frequently (but briefly), then children will often begin to use the terms themselves.

Generalisations – not rules

In a language which is the result of 'overlaying, for nearly a thousand years, of one tradition upon another' (Scragg, 1975, p. 14) it is generally not advisable to teach children so-called rules about our language. In my opinion, it is far better to teach generalisations which have exceptions to them. Two common generalisations which are often taught as rules are considered here.

Firstly, there is the 'magic E' (as it is often termed). Some teachers find it useful in both reading and spelling instruction to show children how the letter *e* at the end of words changes the preceding vowel sound from a short to a long sound. Thus we have: hat/hate, mat/mate, pin/pine, fin/fine, and so on. However, as many teachers know, there are many exceptions to this generalisation in words such as stare, compare, one, done, there, where, have, live, prove, none, come, some. As long as it is not taught as a rule, then novice readers and writers may find the 'magic E' helpful.

It may interest readers to know that the anomaly of the final *e* manifested itself long ago, though as we saw in Chapter 2, since spellings were often dependent on individual choice before the seventeenth century, it did not cause any problems. As Scragg (1975, p. 80) notes, the use of a final *e* as a device for noting vowel length (especially in monosyllabic words such as mate, mete, mute) has its roots in an eleventh-century sound-change involving the lengthening of short vowels. For example, the word *name* was pronounced with a short first vowel sound and with its final *e* sounded; it was thus a disyllabic word then (as were many other words which are now monosyllabic). The final unstressed *e* ceased to be pronounced after the fourteenth century and paved the way for the association of a mute final *e* in spelling with a preceding long vowel. However, after the loss of the final *e* in speech, writers used it in a quite haphazard way, and in books of the sixteenth century *e* was added to almost every word which would otherwise have ended in a consonant. This *ad hoc* use of *e* is illustrated in Scragg's reference to a statement made by the historian, William Camden (1605):

> . . . it hath beene seene where tenne English writing the same sentence, have all concurred, that mong them all there hath beene no other difference than the adding, or omitting once or twice of, our silent E in the end of some wordes. (1974, p. 70)

However, Richard Mulcaster, author of *The First Part of the Elementarie* (1582) had already proposed a regularisation of the final *e*, and in the seventeenth century its use was gradually restricted to words in which it still survives today, though some of the earlier and somewhat haphazard use of the final *e* remains in our language (Scragg, 1974, p. 80). This was evident in the list of exceptions noted previously.

Another 'rule' used by some teachers is the chant '*i* before *e* except after *c*'. Many adult learners recite this quite proudly since it appears to be evidence of their past learning and recall. In my opinion, to teach '*i* before *e*', even as a generalisation, is quite pointless since there are so many common exceptions (for example, height, weight, sleigh, neigh, neighbour, rein, reign, Sheila, Keith). I find it better to teach 'ie' and 'ei' words as they occur in children's work along with other examples in that 'family'. For example, 'My friend is in a field with a piece of pie', or 'Tell me your height and weight before you go on the sleigh, Sheila.' However, I have found that teaching 'ei after c' may be helpful: deceive, deceit, receive (though its usefulness is dependent on the writer knowing that the letter 'c' is required, and not the letter 's').

A further generalisation which may be useful for some children is the observation that many words of more than one syllable which have an 'ik' sound at the end, end in 'ic', for example: basic, critic, automatic, fantastic, electric, athletic, music. (Though for children to be able to use this generalisation, they do need to know what is meant by a syllable.)

David Crystal (1990, p. 72), however, maintains that the 'spelling rules' upon which our spelling system is based may be very helpful to novice spellers despite the fact that there are some exceptions to most of them. He goes on to cite, for example, the common confusion caused by the question of whether to use one consonant or two when adding -*ing* to verbs that end in a consonant, such as *hop* and *sit*; often children write *hoping* for *hopping*, or vice versa. Crystal maintains that the basic rule is simple, as long as the link between spelling and pronunciation is pointed out; thus, the consonant sound is spelled with a double letter if the verb contains one of the short vowels, and it is kept single if the verb contains a long vowel. For example:

Short vowels	*Long vowels*
hop, hopping	hope, hoping
can, canning	mean, meaning
bet, betting	beat, beating

As he acknowledges, though, it is essential that the learners must be able to distinguish between long and short vowels, and I have found that this is not always easy for novice spellers. Indeed, this information has resulted in spellings like *dreamming* and *shoutting*. Moreover, Crystal goes on to point out that when words of more than one syllable are introduced, we have to hear whether the preceding syllable is stressed or not. If it is, there is usually doubling; if it isn't, there isn't (1990, p. 73.) For Example:

occur, occurring	enter, entering
patrol, patrolling	visit, visiting

I have found that, though these rules are generally of great interest to those who are already good spellers, they need very explicit teaching to be helpful to most novice spellers.

Words from other languages

As we saw in Chapter 2, our language is a rich mixture of words from many other countries (or to put it more eloquently, if not more plainly, there is great etymological diversity in our vocabulary). Junior children in particular are often very responsive when made aware of the many words which we use daily and have come to us from other countries. If such awareness is linked with information regarding the origins of our language, then children may themselves become interested in language *per se*. Moreover, information about the source of words in our vocabulary often gives children insights into spellings which may seem unusual (and/or illogical). Of course, such information is best linked to class work, though the influence of other languages upon our own could be taken as a topic in its own right, especially with years 5 and 6.

The suggestions for vocabulary study which follow are but a few of those which teachers may wish to discuss with their classes and, of course, teachers interested in language will want to construct their own and more relevant lists.

Words from the French language

As we saw in Chapter 2, after the coming of William of Normandy in 1066, the French language greatly influenced our own Anglo-Saxon English, and for many years (certainly until the end of the twelfth century), French was regarded as a language of prestige, and those who spoke it generally regarded themselves as 'superior'. One main effect of this bilingualism in England was that a large proportion of present-day English vocabulary is derived from French; Scragg (1975) states:

> A dictionary count might put it as high as forty per cent, though the number of French borrowings in the average English sentence is much smaller because most of the basic and commonest words are English (ie inherited from Old English). (p. 40)

Que endings in our words often indicate the French influence, for example: antique, discothèque, technique, unique. Similarly, words containing *ch* with the soft 'sh' sound are often French in origin, for example: brochure, chauffeur, champagne (sparkling wine, and also a region in eastern France), chantilly (lace or ice-cream; Chantilly is near Paris), chef, machine, parachute.

Children may also be interested in words relating to foods and cooking which are French in origin. For example, café (cf. Nescafé), buttery (a common word seen in colleges, etc. and denoting a place where provisions are kept and supplied), beef (*boeuf*), menu, pork (*porc*), restaurant, veal (*veel*).

Words from the Greek language

The revival of Greek learning in western Europe in the sixteenth century opened up a new source of enrichment for the English vocabulary. As was stated in Chapter 2, since Greek has always been noted for its lucidity and precision, it is not surprising that much of our technical vocabulary is made up of Greek compound words or words derived from Greek; they are in evidence among the following:

Tele (meaning 'far' or 'distant') is a common prefix to many of our common words, for example: telegraph, telex, telepathy, telephone, telescope, telethon (a compound of *tele* and *thon* from the word *marathon*), television.

Scope is a fairly common suffix to some of our words (*skopein* = to see) and is found in horoscope (*horo* = time), stethoscope (*stethos* = breast), telescope, etc.

Similarly, *pathy* is seen fairly frequently as a suffix and prefix in words such as antipathy, apathy, pathetic, sympathy, telepathy.

The consonantal digraph *ph* with its 'f' sound, generally identifies words as being related to the Greek language, for example: orphan, phantom, pharmacy, philatele, photograph, xylophone (*xulon* is the Greek word for wood).

While the French blend *ch* has a soft sound, the Greek *ch* blend is hard. Thus we have: chorus, chlorine, Christmas, echo, mechanic, orchestra, school, stomach.

Words from Latin

The influence of Latin upon our language was mentioned in Chapter 2, and older juniors may find discussion of Latin prefixes in particular useful in aiding both spelling and word meanings.

Aqua (water); aquamarine, aquarium, aquatic, aqueduct. (Note the *e* in the latter word.) *Bi* (or *bin* before a vowel) (two); bi-centenary, biceps, binary, bi-ped, bi-plane. *Ped* (foot); pedal, pedestal, pedestrian, pedometer. *Sub* (under): subconscious, subdue, sub-editor, submarine, subway. *Uni* (one): unicorn, uniform, unity, unilateral, union, unique, unisex, universe.

If teachers can point out relationships between words and their meanings, then, as has been stated, children may improve not only their spelling skills, but also extend their understanding of words they encounter, and perhaps begin to make educated guesses regarding the meaning of words which are new to them. A similar point is made by Shane Templeton (1974) when arguing the case for retaining our traditional orthography (rather than simplifying our spelling process) and for stressing the visual aspect of print. He states that students who are privy to underlying relationships in words may be able to perceive the logical connections between 'equation' and 'equanimity' if they see these words in print. He goes on to state that instruction which gives 'infant' as a fourth grade word, and 'infancy' as an eighth grade word is to be avoided. Mike Torbe (1978, p. 29) also suggests that every so often teachers should relate words to their roots (irrespective of the words' country of origin), for example: care, careful, carefree; or vary, variety, various.

Discussions regarding the use of different language for different purposes may include studies of the language used by advertisements (especially in magazines and television). Much of the language of advertising (whose aim is always to persuade, though not necessarily to sell) is dominated by short, simple words which have their roots in Old English, since the intention is often to convey immediate understanding in language which is familiar. Thus, for example, words like 'friendly', 'home', 'love', 'our', 'your', are immediately 'accessible' to the target audience of advertisements. Conversely, when, for example, advertisers seek to convince us of their technical expertise in the manufacture of a product, then words tend to be Latinate, French or Greek in origin. Thus, the manufacturers of 'Electrolux' may refer to their 'versatile telescopic extension' and manufacturers of scent may refer to 'an exquisite, provocative perfume' (rather than a 'lovely, arousing smell') (Mudd, 1990a, p. 170).

In my experience, children soon are able to distinguish between the familiar words of Old English origin and the (usually) less-familiar words from other languages. If children's curiosity can be aroused, then they may be led to discover much that is interesting about our language but, as in most teaching, much is dependent upon the teacher's ability to promote and develop curiosity and interest.

Did you know?

As a post-script to the lists of words and word parts from other languages, I have included some information about word origins which teachers may read for their own interest and, by reference to etymological dictionaries, expand on if they wish to help older juniors to acquire knowledge about their language and heritage.

Note: I have included meanings, but some children (perhaps working in groups) may like to guess meanings for themselves.

Bedlam – a madhouse or scene of uproar; it was an abbreviation of the hospital of St Mary of Bethlehem in London and founded in 1547 as an asylum for the insane.

Breakfast – the first meal of the day in which one breaks (interrupts) their 'fast' since the previous day.

Gipsy (gypsy) – a member of a wandering race, speaking a language called Romany. When they first appeared in England in the early sixteenth century, they were thought to come from Egypt because of their dark skin. Their language is, in fact, related to Hindi.

Hippopotamus – a large African tusked, hairless short-legged quadruped inhabiting rivers and thought to resemble a horse as it stood in water. Hence, *hippos*, the Greek word for horse, plus *potamus*, a river.

Holiday – originally this was a day of festivity or recreation when no work was done. It is formed from the Old English words Holy Day (*haligdaeg*).

Journal/journey – are related to the French word *jour* meaning day. A 'journey' was considered to be a day's travel, and a 'journal' refers mainly to daily newspapers.

Ostracise (or -ize) – to exclude from society. The Greek word *ostrakon* means a piece of shell (or potsherd). In ancient Athens, dangerously powerful or unpopular citizens were banished for five or ten years by a voting system in which the name of the person to be ostracised was written on a broken piece of shell.

Daisy – a small wild and garden flower with a yellow centre and white petals. It originates from the Old English words for the day's eye, since the centre was revealed in the morning.

Tulip – a spring-flowering plant; from the Turkish *tulband* and the Persian *dulband* (turban) which describes the shape of the expanded flower.

(The origins of *salary* and *denim* may interest some children; these were discussed earlier in this chapter, pages 152 and 153.)

Copying

Many references have been made already to the avoidance of 'blind' copying; however, as has been stated, too, there is, in my opinion, a place for the thoughtful copying of texts which interest children, and which may have been chosen by them. Graves (1983) and Beard (1984) both consider that a range of 'quality' literature and poetry may not only stimulate children's love of language, but also provide them with a range of models upon which to base their own writing. It is thus suggested that sometimes children be allowed to copy out their own sections from poetry, prose, songs, etc., and, if they wish, to illustrate the writing. Such work could form the basis for personal anthology books (which could be retained throughout the junior school and would be an ideal method of recording their changing 'tastes' in literature).

Beard referred also to the use of jokes and puns as one means of helping children to become interested in language. Similarly, I have used amusing and brief extracts from copies of the *Readers' Digest* with children to explain the function of punctuation, including, in particular, inverted commas, questions and exclamation marks. During the time given to compiling anthologies, some children have chosen to include one or more of these amusing anecdotes. (It should be noted though that sometimes these anecdotes require explanation and discussion before they are appreciated by all the members of the class.) Note, too, that children often need regular reminders regarding 'thoughtful' copying in which they try to recall some words/phrases from memory. They may also need reminding about checking their work for accuracy (checking is often successfully carried out if done in twos). Moreover, copying may be combined with occasional but regular instruction in handwriting so that children are reminded about correct letter formation.

Testing spellings

We have seen that educationalists such as Schonell (1942), Peters (1985) and Graves (1983) all agree that, ideally, spelling instruction should be given daily (albeit very briefly). Indeed, Graves considers that spelling instruction given once a week is virtually useless, and that brief daily instruction enables teachers to discuss spellings in relation to the children's

work. Moreover, I consider that teachers also need to check that children who find spelling difficult are really understanding instruction given as opposed to *thinking* that what is being taught is being learned. Regular testing (which need not be stressful if it is directed at the different levels of ability within a class) may help the children as well as the teachers to monitor progress and difficulties/misunderstandings. Fridays seem ideal days for tests to be given (though teachers may have other ideas about this).
The main point is that they should be given on a specific day of the week so that the children get into the routine of preparing for tests on a regular basis. Teachers should include the spellings in sentences and, if possible, in continuous text so that the children experience flow of writing; also, it helps to reinforce and revise children's knowledge of spellings if past work is included in dictated texts.

As in the section on testing in years 1 and 2 in Chapter 7, it is intended to assume that classes are divided into three main groups: above average, average and below average in writing skills; similarly (as with younger children), teachers may refer to the groups by names chosen by the children themselves (and these may vary from names of 'pop' stars to nearby districts). In order to give examples of tests at three levels of ability, I shall assume that the class of 8- and 9-year-old children, who wrote about their first day at school, were given tests based on class discussions and their written work.

Younger children may be allowed to select their own words for learning after year 3; however, I consider that teachers should make the selection based upon classwork as a *general* rule. Words to be learned may be entered into personal dictionaries with an abbreviation of the date written in brackets, for example: although (9 Oct).

The above average group's words might include: rough, cough, although, though, thought, McGough; photocopy, photocopies, photocopier, computer, word-processor; excite, excited, excitement.

The number of words given may vary between, for example, 10–20 for this group. Since some of the children had used direct speech in their work, but in some cases were unclear of the use of inverted commas, the sentences could include some direct speech. Thus, sentences given to this group might be:

    1   I thought that the teacher had made photocopies of the poem by McGough.

2 My mother said, 'You can play with the baby, although you must not be rough with him because he has a bad cough.'

3 When I saw a word-processor and a computer in our classroom, I was excited.

Note that, ideally, sentences should not contain 'extra' words which are likely to be difficult for the children to spell; if, however, 'new' words are necessary to make sentences more interesting, then the teacher may display them visually for the children.

The average group might be asked to learn: McGough, rough, cough, thought; scared, arrived, turned (some of the children in the group had omitted 'e' from the 'ed' suffix); playground, sound, found, fountain, mountain.

A 'text' given to this group might be: When I arrived at the playground, I found a water-fountain. As I turned it on, it made a splashing sound. In the classroom, I thought that I could not read the poem by McGough because I had a cough.

Punctuation would be given to this group; also, the new words, 'splashing', 'poem', 'because', would be displayed for the children to refer to if necessary.

The below average group's spellings might include some high-frequency words which are still proving difficult to remember. I would also include one or two words chosen by them. Thus, their learning might include: some, come, home, came, name, same, does, goes, friends, McGough (the latter two words being their choice, perhaps).

Sentences for this group might be:

1 I come to school with some friends. When the bell goes, I go home with my friends.

2 My name is the same as his (hers), but s/he does not like his/ her name.

The children would be helped with respect to punctuation and the use of capital letters. Also, the word *school* would be displayed for the children to refer to. It is essential that spellings to be included in tests are revised regularly along with any other instruction so that the children are helped in their learning tasks. Moreover, so that past learning is consolidated, it is a good idea to have tests (perhaps half-termly) which are based on past spellings and instruction. On the actual day of testing, the groups may be tested at 'staggered' intervals so that they get on with other pieces of work (including reading) until it is time for their test. It is suggested that each sentence is read clearly before the children begin to write. At the end of the test, the sentences may be read again, fairly slowly, so that children may check for omissions. Teachers may collect in books or jotters from each group as they finish and then move on to the next group. When all groups have finished (and this may take only 15–20 minutes) teachers may distribute books/jotters to children from the same group so that the children can mark each other's work. The sentences could be written on the board and covered by a large paper which may be removed as children are ready to mark. Of course, some boards are not fixed, and thus dictations could be written on the back of them until required.

It is essential that teachers are clear about how the work is marked; I do not give the children marks out of a specified total, instead I prefer the markers to underline any incorrect spellings so that children may easily correct their own work, and also evaluate the extent of their progress. Misspellings may be re-entered into personal dictionaries (using the Look/ Cover – Write/Check method). It is a good idea to make some time for brief discussions about how the children consider that they have fared in their tests. Any common difficulties may be noted, and discussed then or at a later date.

Note that children who are very good spellers may have no problems with work set for the above-average group; they may be interested in undertaking some dictionary and/or etymological studies of their own (or studies set by the teacher) to add to their collection of words in their personal dictionaries, and perhaps shared later with some of the other children. Children who evidence severe spelling difficulties will be considered in the next chapter.

It should be stressed that regular instruction need only take a small proportion of each (if possible) school day. Moreover, it should give most children a solid base upon which to improve the quality of their writing skills without having to interrupt their train of thought constantly due to concern about the correctness of their spellings. Confidence in spelling ability gives self-esteem to the writer and, in particular, to junior children who soon become aware they are poor spellers. Some teachers may maintain that such testing reinforces any lack of confidence in writing; my response is that if tests are adjusted to the children's capabilities, then they can only help the children to note their progress at their level since they are not trying to compete with other children. I also maintain that children who dislike writing and groan as it is suggested, are often the victims of inadequate instruction and help in spelling.

Strange as it may seem at first, my opinion is, I think, not disproved by Joan Jones' (1988) account of regular spelling instruction and tests given to third year juniors; she reported that after a year the children showed no real progress in spelling, though there were exceptional gains in their reading quotients. The first point that I would make is that the work was undertaken in the first place to remedy the many basic errors found in their writing (Jones, 1988, p. 25). Also, no mention was made of organising different work for different groups, the weekly list was prepared by the teacher and related to spelling patterns (for example, *al, ay, able, tion*), which Jones considered that the children ought to have covered. Also it appears that tests were upon words and not sentences, 'Regularly, on Friday mornings . . . the week's words were tested' (p. 28). In my opinion, the major problem lay in the fact that apparently no systematic spelling instruction had been given previously and thus no foundations had been laid for the intensive course outlined by Jones which, moreover, gave no consideration to the different needs of the children in the class.

Interestingly, the children's improved reading quotients did lead Jones to wonder if the time spent in systematic consideration of common blends in words had helped to improve the children's phonological strategies (p. 30). Goswami and Bryant (1990, p. 148) noted in their research that children's phonological knowledge is not always utilised in their early stages of reading. It is likely that Jones' instruction (as she suggests) promoted this improvement in reading.

Once children have shown themselves to be confident in their knowledge of the 'basics' of spelling, testing may be abandoned; and for some children, provided that the groundwork has been started in the infant school (and continued), this occurs during or before their fifth year in school.

Record-keeping

Teachers' records of children's progress and difficulties in spelling are essential if, as has been suggested, teachers relate spelling to class work rather than 'set' lists (like Schonell's) which move in sequence through various blends of letters, silent letters, suffixes, etc. I would suggest that while there is no 'set sequence' for learning about our orthography, teachers do need to refer regularly to work covered and check it against their spelling aims for the year in order to ascertain that no important instruction is being overlooked. Records may be kept in one notebook and, if used daily as teachers interact with the children, its 'upkeep' should prove a relatively easy task. Each child may be allocated two or three pages of the book – alphabetically sequenced for ease of location. (Records of dictations set may be kept in a separate notebook.) Moreover, the children's personal dictionaries should, provided the children have been encouraged to use them regularly, provide a valuable source of any specific difficulties encountered by the class, groups or individuals, and may enable teachers to give appropriate remediation where necessary.

Of course, spelling instruction is only a part of the writing process; it is also vital that teachers keep records of the children's written work, and their attitudes to the work in order to mark progress and identify needs. The National Curriculum in English (Gathering Evidence of Achievements, E1:11) states:

> The recording of children's progress in writing needs to include drafts of writing as well as completed writing. It is useful to record how the child tackles writing, revises text, and discusses and reflects on it. Samples of children's writing should be collected over a key stage so that development and range can be monitored. Writing is an area where children can be involved in self-assessment, discussing and commenting on their work.

Spelling attainment by the end of years 5 and 6

The following attainment targets are taken from 'English in the National Curriculum' and include also targets which should have been reached before the end of year 2. Pupils should be able to:

- Produce recognisable (though not necessarily always correct) spelling of a range of common words (2a).

- Spell correctly, in the course of their own writing, simple monosyllabic words they use regularly which observe common patterns, for example: see, car, man, sun, hot, cold, thank (2b).

- Recognise that spelling has patterns, and begin to apply their knowledge of those patterns in their attempts to spell a wider range of words, for example: coat, goat, feet, street (2c).

- Show knowledge of the names and order of the letters of the alphabet (2d).

- Spell correctly, in the course of their own writing, simple polysyllabic words they use regularly which observe common patterns, for example: because, after, open, teacher, animal, together (3a).

- Recognise and use correctly regular patterns for vowel sounds and common letter strings, for example: -ing, -ion, -ous (3b).

- Show a growing awareness of word families and their relationships, for example: grow, growth, growing, grown, grow (3c).

- In revising and redrafting their writing, begin to check the accuracy of their spelling – use a simple dictionary, word book, spell checker, or other classroom resources; make spelling books or picture books (3d).

The programmes of study for writing, spelling and handwriting in the National Curriculum suggest, too, that in the context of their own writing, pupils may be introduced to grammatical terms such as sentence, verb, tense, noun or pronoun (Peters (1985) noted that studies of irregular past tenses are often missing from manuals on spelling instruction).

- Spell correctly, in the course of their own writing, words which display other main patterns in English spelling – words using the main prefixes and suffixes, for example: dis-, un-, in-, im-, il-, ir-, -ed, -ary, -ible, -able, -ness, -ful (4a).

Also, it is often helpful to illustrate to children how the roots of words (or morphemes, which are the smallest meaningful units of language) may change meaning and function if a prefix and/or suffix is added. For example: un*thank*ful; dis*appear*ed; im*possible*.

Studies of the influence of other languages upon our own should introduce junior children gradually to a wide and useful range of the meanings of prefixes (and suffixes) and could include: bi-, tri-, cent-, tele-, syn-, -ology, pre-, mis-, sur-, sub-, ex-, inter-, semi-.

Summary

There have been many suggestions put forward about spelling in this and the previous chapter which may apparently contradict ideas formulated by some teachers, possibly during their own schooldays; and this may apply especially to teachers who believe in asking children to sound out words which they wish to spell. Like Peters, I consider that many children (especially juniors) are at a disadvantage 'as long as they rely for their spelling on pronunciation' (Peters, 1985, p. 34). Therefore, the main stress in this book has been on teaching/helping children to look carefully at words to be learned, though it is acknowledged that some privileged children have 'photographic' memories and thus seldom need to study words in order to recall them. It is also acknowledged that in the early stages of learning to spell, most children need to be able to relate symbols to sounds in order to gain 'access' to our spelling system.

Stress too has been upon continual reminders that children should not become 'blind' copiers of words and text, but rather that they should become responsible for their own learning and checking for accuracy as they make use of a variety of spelling resources.

The teacher is at the centre of most effective learning, and success therefore depends largely on the teacher's own knowledge about spelling. Since some students in initial teacher training freely admit that they are poor spellers, I can only assume that there is a significant number of teachers (ex-students) who are also poor spellers. I urge such teachers to do something about it as soon as possible and, perhaps with the help of a colleague, they could pin-point spellings which are causing difficulties and, possibly, using some of the methods described, remedy the situation, bearing in mind the maxim 'a little and often'.

Moreover, teachers (and head teachers) should ensure that there is adequate planning of the spelling syllabus, with regular contact between teachers (and especially between infant and junior departments) to discuss methodology. It is clearly vital, too, that teachers keep records of spelling instruction given as well as records of individual progress and difficulties.

However, despite the ideas suggested for regular and structured spelling instruction based on ongoing lessons, there is no guarantee that *all* the children in a class will achieve their spelling potential; there may be some children who experience quite severe difficulties in learning to spell. As Wade and Wedell (1974) state: 'it is not possible to give teachers a *universal* key to spelling skills which can be passed on to pupils' (my emphasis; p. 9). But what teachers can do is to give most children confidence in themselves as people and writers and a sound base for developing their writing skills. It is thus hoped that some of the suggestions in this book help more teachers to do just that, as they combine the best of traditional instruction with the best of more recent educational philosophies and also their existing expertise as teachers.

As a final (and lighter) point for reflection, before moving on to consider children with spelling difficulties, I would like to recount a story (possibly apocryphal) recalled by Mick Water at a meeting held at Edge Hill College in 1992. He told of an inspector in English visiting a class of junior children who had been writing poetry for the teacher. He had been looking at several children's poems in their exercise books when his attention was caught by the poem in one boy's book. Picking up the book, the inspector read the poem aloud:

> War war war
> Armies armies armies
> Firing firing firing
> Death death death

'That's a very good poem,' said the inspector, 'it has a strong, effective rhythm.' The reply came, 'Sir, it's not my poem, it's my spelling corrections from last week.'

9 *Children with spelling difficulties*

Peters (1985) and Todd (1982) consider that systematic and relevant instruction in spelling should help the majority of children to achieve functional competence; I fully endorse their opinions. However, as stated in the previous two chapters, there is no single method of helping *all* children to become effective spellers (and writers); there will inevitably be some children who need specific remedial help because of difficulties arising from a variety (and possibly a combination) of causes. It is thus intended to consider some probable causes of difficulties and to suggest some methods of remediation.

Who are the spellers with difficulties?

In the chapter on assessing spelling, it was argued that children whose spelling miscues evidenced their knowledge not only of sound/symbol correspondence, but also of common spelling patterns, would, with appropriate instruction, soon be on the way to becoming effective spellers. (For example, children who write 'beleave' for 'believe', or 'spase' for 'space'.) Children whose spelling miscues do not conform to common spelling patterns ('qeshun' for 'question', or 'cof' for 'cough'), but who spell according to sound/symbol correspondence, need (as Peters continually stresses) their attention to be drawn to the visual aspects of print and to be helped to an awareness of common letter patterns in our language; they also need to be weaned away from spelling only according to sound. Again, with appropriate and regular instruction, these children should become competent spellers. Children whose spellings occasionally evidence mis-hearing or mis-pronunciation (perhaps due to their dialect, for example, some*think* for some*thing*) will often be able to remedy their misspellings after hearing the word pronounced correctly (several times) and seeing the word in print.

However, there are some children whose spellings appear quite bizarre, evidencing deficits with respect to sound/symbol relationships and/or recall of sound sequences, and/or hearing sounds correctly, and/or recall of visual letter patterns. These children, even at junior stages, may be writing 'chidern' for 'children', 'thug' for 'took', 'naslon' for 'neatly', 'frit' for 'first', or 'anuer' for 'another'. Additionally, these children may vary the same spellings from day to day, even getting them right on occasions! Of course, one could argue that these children should have been detected and helped much earlier in their school life, but given multiple variables, such as children changing school, children being absent for long or short periods, illness of teachers and changeover of staff within a school, we just have to supply regular help as soon as possible, and the help needs also to be structured, brief and with only a few children.

Sound/symbol deficits

There was stress in the preceding chapters on the visual aspects of words in the spelling process, and Peters (1985) suggests that children who apparently have no spelling strategies (like, I suppose, the child who wrote 'naslon' for 'neatly') should be taken back to the earliest stages of spelling (involving Look/Cover – Write/Check methods) with stress upon the visual, and using their names and addresses as starting points. Here I disagree with Peters to some extent, since I consider that in the earliest stages of learning to spell (no matter what the age), learners need to know the relationship between sounds of the alphabet and their written form. Bryant's and Bradley's research (1985, p. 20) has led them to suggest that young children's spelling 'depends very closely on letter sound correspondences'. Similarly, though arguing the importance of motor and visual abilities in the spelling process, Peters also acknowledges that 'Obviously a child must be able to hear and discriminate letter sounds' (1975, p. 11).

Moreover, although as effective adult readers we do not normally use sound/symbol correspondence as we read, we do *have* this knowledge and we use it actively as we 'decipher' children's (and adults') earlier attempts at writing, for example, as we interpret 'tchoolipps' (tulips) or 'njun' (engine). Similarly, we saw that as children's knowledge of letter sound correspondences increases, their invented spellings become more sophisticated, and gradually teachers are able to help children to acquire more knowledge (via visual attention) regarding common letter strings in our traditional orthography – but the point to remember is that these children *first* used letter sound correspondence to help them in their spellings. Thus, I think that children experiencing spelling difficulties need to have their knowledge of sound/symbol correspondence checked in order to help them to make their first deductions about our written process. It is important also to check that sounds of all the letters of the alphabet are known, since I have found that many children with spelling difficulties do not know *all* the letter sounds. Indeed, Peters (1993), when writing about spelling intervention for children with spelling difficulties, states that: 'Intervention should occur when phonological knowledge is secure' (p. 185). Of course, such teaching needs to be done in brief but regular stages; also, the sequence of learning the letter sounds may vary from child to child.

Initial letters of some children's names and addresses may be very useful (as suggested in Chapter 7) for relating knowledge about letter sounds to themselves. However, since names and addresses are often irregular in terms of sound/symbol correspondence, I would discuss (in early remedial instruction) only regular initial letters of names/addresses and teach regular letter strings, such as: an, and, at, bat, hat. However, names such as Ann(e), Alan, Helen, Jack, Tom, lend themselves very well to instruction on sound letter correspondence and teachers may use them as a base for gradually extending knowledge of letter strings. For example:

Ann	and	Helen	Jack	Tom
an	ant	held	back	top
can	band	help	mack	toss
fan	hand	lend	pack	tot
pan	land	lent	rack	atom (if of interest,
man	sand		sack	and its meaning is
				explained)

If children are ready, high-frequency but irregular words may be added to such lists (for example, 'he/she' may be added to the third column, and 'to' may be added to the fifth column.

Judith Wright and Asher Cashdan spoke about planned strategies for readers with difficulties at the United Kingdom Reading Association (UKRA) Conference at Edge Hill College in 1989, and though they concentrated on reading, their references to structured tuition and to the use of plastic letters has often proved useful in helping children with spelling difficulties. Similarly, Bryant and Bradley (1985, p. 76) state that less able readers (and in my experience, this applies to spellers, too) are often successful in the aural medium which to them seems particularly abstract and transitory. It is Bradley's experience, 'that they are helped if, as they are being taught about sound categories, they are given something concrete and tangible to work with'. If we consider again the name Ann (Anne) or the 'an' blend, and include the use of plastic letters in spelling instruction, we see that the 'an' blend is common to them both. Thus, the plastic letters 'an' should remain static while the letters which form other words are placed in front or behind them by the teacher and then by the child/ren.

Bryant and Bradley add (p. 76) that in addition to helping children to see the relationship between sound and letters, alliteration and/or rhyme may become literally tangible. (Similar methods were discussed when working with infants in Chapter 7.) As has been stated previously, Bryant and Bradley think that 'many children with learning difficulties are insensitive to rhyme and alliteration' (p. ix).

Moreoever, Lynette Bradley (1990) restated the belief that if children realise very early on that rhyming words often have similar letter patterns, then this usually means that they have found a way to reduce the number of words they have to learn. They only need to remember one word from each rhyming category. This will leave more working memory free to deal with words which must be remembered individually because of their unusual letter patterns (people, because, etc.). She considers that children get better at remembering letter strings and spelling words if they have some way to organise the task (p. 96). Bradley also stresses the need for teachers to help children to make the connections between alliteration (onset) and rhyme (rime) in spoken words and in print since children with spelling and reading difficulties appear to be particularly insensitive to these connections. She states:

> If children do not hear the connections then every word they need to read or spell is a unique word, and the task of learning them must seem overwhelming. It must be like having to learn every word in a dictionary without any way of organising the task, no way to begin except to choose a word and learn it, and then take any other word, and learn that, and so on. (p. 86)

It must be stated, though, that Bryant and Bradley do acknowledge the possibility that insensitivity to alliteration and rhyme are not necessarily the *causes* of reading and writing failure since it may be that children improve in their sensitivity to alliteration and rhyme as they improve in reading and writing. Their studies, however, do indicate that children experiencing difficulties in learning to read and write benefit from training in the detection of rhyme and alliteration.

Wright and Cashdan (1989) (UKRA Conference) also stressed the importance of teachers saying words as they are formed, and encouraging the children to repeat the words. Similarly, I think that since we are concerned with children being able to spell words from memory, they could be encouraged to say letter names as they form the words. When teachers feel that children are ready, they could be introduced to attempting their first learning by the Look/Cover – Write/Check method, but in the case of these children, a multi-sensory approach may be adopted whereby the children go through the following stages:

1   look at the word, say the word and then its letters in sequence;

2   'write' it in the air with eyes closed saying the whole word first, then the letters;

3   write it on a desk (or in wet sand) saying the word first and the letters while doing so (then, if all appears to be correct to the teacher);

4   write the word on paper (saying the word, then the letters while doing so).

I suggest that if the word is correct, the child is allowed to put ticks over each correct letter and add an extra tick if all the letters are in the correct order. Thus 'Jack' would receive five ticks, one for each correct letter, and one for the correct sequence. A child writing 'Jakc' would receive four ticks, and his or her attention would be drawn to the 'ck' sequence. If the word is incorrect, the process may be repeated provided that the child is not showing signs of stress. Usually, though, if the above procedures are carried out carefully, children are often successful. Also, it is a good idea to allow the child to role play being the teacher (recommended by Wright and Cashdan (1989)). I suggest that the children write the word in the air, then on the board (or paper) for the teacher to copy, talking about their thought processes as they do so. Of course, children often find such 'talking aloud' rather difficult at first, but if encouraged to do it gradually, teachers are often able to identify particular confusions which the children may be experiencing and thus supply appropriate remediation.

Thus, my initial recommendations for children who evidence bizarre spelling miscues are that they be introduced to the regularities of our language (after having checked that they know the letter names and sounds of our alphabet). Once they have experienced some measure of success with a number of regular spelling patterns, and are perhaps able to write several words with confidence, they may be introduced to a few relevant, high-frequency, irregular spellings, for example: to, go, so, do, my, by, all, call, some, come. These spellings may be learned gradually with other words in the same 'visual family' using the Look/Cover – Write/Check method. Very brief dictations (perhaps just one sentence at first) may then be given, with the child deciding how many words he or she wishes to learn, and the teacher helping to decide *which* words to learn. A typical dictated sentence for a child experiencing spelling difficulties might (after two or three weeks) be: 'I am Jack and I go back to pack my bag', or 'I can go (out) to play with my bat and my ball.' As before, teachers may display any extra words which might make dictated sentences more relevant (and interesting) to the child. If children are interested enough, they often surprise us by succeeding unexpectedly in some learning tasks.

It is worthy of note that dictated passages play an important part in Clay's assessments for reading recovery programmes (1981 and 1990). She states (1981, p. 26) that simple sentences are dictated clearly to children and in the marking they are given credit for every *sound* written correctly, even though the word may be spelled uncorrectly. Clay goes on to say that dictations are useful indications of the child's ability to go from analysis of sounds in spoken words to written forms which represent the sounds. In that sense they are, of course, not 'true' dictations or spelling tests.

Once children are making good progress in their spelling, they often wish to learn longer and more complex words of relevance to them. When this stage is reached, they may find it easier if, as suggested by Sassoon (1990, p. 13) and Moseley (1974, p. 21) words are broken up into syllables (or smaller sections). It is usually the middle part of longer words that are omitted or confused by children who do not find spelling easy. However, I do *not* suggest that words are separated by lines which may distort the visual image (for example, tele/vi/sion); though teachers may, after saying the whole word clearly and not too quickly, decide (in consultation with the child) where the word may be divided aurally. The way in which a word is 'broken' depends very much upon the individual learner. Interestingly, a 17-year-old student of mine with spelling difficulties, wanted to learn to spell the word 'technology' correctly after having made several incorrect attempts at the word. After looking at the word carefully, he divided it most unexpectedly into: tec hno logy. He was a chemistry student and HNO was familiar to him as nitrous acid. When writing the word, he would say the syllable *tec*, then the individual letters *hno*, and finally the word part, *logy*. In this way, he was using auditory and visual strategies together with a relevant association to help him to recall the visual form of the word.

Similarly, children who have experienced difficulties in learning to spell may be encouraged to develop their own mnemonics for some of the words they wish to learn. (Mnemonics were discussed in Chapter 8.)

Motivating children with spelling difficulties

A further and relevant point made by Todd (1982, p. 95) is that older children who find spelling very difficult are more likely to feel failures and to be negative in their attitude towards remedial instruction. She considers that sometimes an approach which includes the use of some 'novelty' equipment may help to motivate children to practise new learning. For example, she suggests the use of typewriters (if available) or the use of coloured pens/pencils. More recently, word-processors and computers have become readily available in many schools. Todd feels that such equipment may give high status to the writing process, since the work produced is clear, professional and, moreover, the left-to-right sequence of writing is reinforced. However, as she admits, one has to remember that children do need to be taught the use of space bars, shifts, etc., and also they need to consider the layout of keyboards which are not alphabetical (this is in order that those letters which are used a lot are positioned in an accessible place to facilitate speedy typing). It occurs to me that if the use of a typewriter (or any other type of technical equipment) is practical, then when children's spelling improves, their attention may be drawn to common letter groups, such as 'er', 'ere', 'th', 'tion', etc.

Todd suggests that children be allowed to type with any fingers since they are not being taught to type, and that 20 minutes of typing time is sufficient. Common words may be tried first, followed perhaps by the sentence they are learning for dictation or, as Todd suggests, simple instructions for use in the class, such as 'Please turn off the lights', or 'Please close the door.' Naturally, the child may make incorrect attempts at such labels; this does not matter as long as the child is allowed to judge his or her own work and select the best for class use. I must admit that I do have reservations about the lack of 'flow' which accompanies the novice typist, yet I do know that typewriters, etc., are able to provide motivation for some reluctant writers who lack confidence; also the desire to want to do something sometimes means that the 'battle' may be more than half won.

Once confidence has been restored, the child should return to traditional methods of writing with the teacher assuring the child that this return is a sign of progress and success.

179

Visual memory deficits

In the Look/Cover – Write/Check method of learning spelling, stress is mainly on visual memory as children revisualise letters seen and transfer them to written form. Yet as Anne Marshall-Huston (1991) says, 'any child in the classroom may have poor visual memory and need remediation' (p. 177). Among suggestions for remediation are multi-sensory techniques (like the ones referred to earlier in this chapter), and also ones which encourage children to use their fingers to trace words written in black on white surfaces, or to trace words/sentences which are glued on card to raise the surface, saying the words aloud as they do so. Marshall-Huston also recommends games such as 'Fish' and 'Hiding the Object'. The first is a game in which cards containing letters or words are placed on a table face down; the children then take turns in turning over a card and trying to locate its 'twin' on the table. If a match is made, the child may keep the pair of cards and continue until no match is made. If there is no match, the child replaces the card trying to retain the letters of words in his or her memory; he or she should also try to recall where he or she replaced the card; another child then takes a turn. The second game is one in which five (more or less) familiar objects are placed on a tray and covered with a cloth. As the children gather round the tray, the teacher explains that the children should look carefully at the objects and try to remember everything they see. They may be given 5 (more or less) seconds to do this and then the tray should be re-covered. The children then try to recall what they have seen. In an alternative version, one object may be removed (without the children seeing its removal); they may then try to guess what has been removed from the tray.

Such methods, particularly when used with young children, may help to improve visual recall, although I do have some reservations regarding the extent to which they will succeed as *remedial* methods if teachers do not actively and explicitly help children to develop strategies for remembering objects placed on a tray. I suggest, therefore, that if, for example, a pen, pencil, piece of paper, crayon and small notebook are placed on a tray, then the children may be encouraged to group/link together objects which seem to 'go' together. Thus, they may link mentally the three writing implements (pen, pencil, crayon) and the two materials for writing on (paper, notebook); it should be fairly simple then to recall any object which is removed. With respect to the game 'Fish' (which I think is more difficult for children with poor visual memories), teachers may need to show children how to recall word positions; they may be encouraged to think aloud, for example, that 'cat' is the end card near the top of the tray and on the left (even if the concept names of: top, end, bottom, left, right, etc., are not known by a child, they are usually able to differentiate these directions without actually naming them). Moreover, I think it essential that only a few cards are used with children in the initial stages of improving visual memory.

Summary

In summary, then, teachers of children experiencing difficulties in spelling should try to locate the specific source of difficulty and supply appropriate instruction in (preferably) a combination of two or more of the following areas:

- sound/symbol correspondence of the English language, including names of letters of the alphabet;

- common and regular letter strings which may include the use of plastic letters;

- awareness of irregular but high-frequency words in which the visual aspects of the words is studied;

- clear articulation of words to be studied and also clear articulation of the letters of the words (in sequence);

- multi-sensory approaches to the Look/Cover – Write/Check methods of learning spellings;

- relevant games to aid visual memory deficits;

- use of mnemonics to aid learning;

- possible use of typewriters to aid motivation in learning;

- very brief informal tests on one or two sentences which contain words learned – the aim is to ensure the child's success.

This brings us full circle in teaching children with difficulties in spelling; such children generally need to be shown *how* to look carefully at words and, as has been stated many times already, teachers should show by example how to study new words to be learned and pick out what, for them, is likely to be a difficult part of the word. Moreover, children who have experienced difficulties in their spelling are likely to need even more careful and explicit instruction in this routine than children who find knowledge about our spelling system relatively easy to assimilate.

We must remember, too, that there will be some children who have such severe mental auditory and visual deficits that specialist teaching of individuals by outreach teachers is required. What I have tried to do in this chapter is to outline some of the methods by which children requiring remedial help in spelling may be encouraged by the *non-specialist* teacher to make progress and, equally important, to gain self-confidence. As was stated in Chapter 7, though, the early detection and early remediation of difficulties (preferably in the top infant class) should mean that children do not reach the stage of feeling a failure. This in itself can become a major barrier to learning of any kind. Indeed, Bradley (1990, p. 83) suggested that we can approach the problem of children's reading and spelling difficulties in two ways: we can identify the nature of the difficulties and develop appropriate teaching strategies to overcome them; or we can try to prevent the problem in the first place. As with any problem, prevention is better than cure.

Book summary

In the first chapter of this book, the National Curriculum was acknowledged as giving status to spelling within the writing process; also its description of levels of attainment through all stages of schooling has provided the basis for standardisation in this subject. What the National Curriculum has not done is to provide teachers with explicit information on how these levels may be achieved and how to detect and help children who fail to achieve them. Nor has it provided teachers with a background of information about our language so that they may understand some of the reasons for some of the irregularities of our spelling system. It is the author's hope that this book has compensated for such omissions in the National Curriculum.

Chapter 2 of this book considered briefly some of the major influences upon our language and our spelling system; the latter has conserved part of the history of our island in it. It is thus regarded as inherently fascinating by some people. However, since our spelling system often reflects the way that some words were pronounced over five hundred years ago, there are also many potential difficulties in it for the novice spellers. Teachers of spelling should benefit from an understanding of some of the causes of such seeming anomalies.

In Chapter 3, the views of researchers specifically interested in spelling and writing were discussed and, at the end of the chapter, consideration was given to children's phonemic and visual awareness in their spelling (and reading). Generally, it was suggested that in the early stages of spelling instruction, children's attention should be drawn to both auditory and visual aspects of print, but that as they become more competent spellers, attention should be concentrated more on the visual rather than the auditory. It was recommended too that early instruction should encourage and help children to be aware of common letter sequences and alliteration and rhyme in their reading and writing. 'Blind' copying was to be discouraged and the visual memorisation of words encouraged. The concensus of opinion was that all spelling instruction should be regular, systematic, brief and relevant to the children's needs and/or ongoing classwork. For all ages of children, one of the main aims was to help children to become increasingly responsible for their own progress in spelling.

Since the ability to spell confidently is only of value within the writing process (that is, it is not an end in itself), Chapter 4 addressed the writing process as a whole. Some of the methods were considered whereby children's ability to express themselves in writing could be promoted and extended.

Children's progress in their ability to express themselves in writing is dependent on teachers firstly assessing their levels of attainment in spelling/writing. Thus, Chapter 5 provided examples of young writers' work (all aged between 5 and 6 years plus); their levels of attainment were discussed and suggestions for helping the children to 'move on' in their writing were also put foward. Praise was given for their positive strategies, and areas of difficulty were discussed with them. This chapter also considered how teachers could detect possible spelling problems very early in their school lives via screening tests, and measure children's progress and/or difficulties up to year 6 by analysing spelling errors.

In Chapter 6, we saw that well-formed handwriting had been linked with spelling ability by some researchers. They believe that correctly-formed, joined writing not only aids the continuous flow of children's work and thoughts, but also that instruction on common letter patterns (including word endings) given in handwriting lessons can build up children's knowledge about the probability of certain letter sequences. Such knowledge may help the spelling of words containing common sequences to become automatic in the children's written work.

Chapter 7 was concerned with practical suggestions for spelling instruction with young children; it was based on educationalists' views discussed mainly in Chapters 3 and 6 and also on the author's experience in teaching spelling. Initial focus was on helping them to become aware of the relationship between the spoken word and print and, in particular, in helping them to identify the names of and sounds of the letters of the alphabet speedily. The correct formation of letters was encouraged via multi-sensory approaches; also the children's own names and nursery rhymes (displayed in written form) were among suggestions for discussions which aimed to promote an interest in literacy.

Practical suggestions for children from year 2 to year 6 were included in Chapter 8. These children were expected to be using an increasingly larger proportion of correctly spelled words in their written work. Recommendations aimed at promoting their effective use of dictionaries and etymological dictionaries were made. Suggestions were also put forward whereby teachers with sufficient background knowledge could discuss words, prefixes, suffixes from other languages – these being an integral part of our vocabulary. As in all spelling instruction, it was stressed that word and letter studies should be related to ongoing work within the class and relevant to the children.

Since the suggestions for instruction in Chapters 7 and 8 were directed at teachers with quite large classes of children, it was considered that invididual instruction was generally not practical. Thus, it was recommended that teachers divided the children into roughly three groups, that is, below average, average and above average.

Of course, there will always be times when some children do need specific and possibly individual help with their work, especially children experiencing difficulties in their spelling. For this reason, Chapter 9 sought to give advice to teachers of children with specific spelling difficulties.

This book then has balanced the *essence* of methods of spelling instruction which have proved successful in the past with what has been learned recently via current research. Methods of instruction have been at class, group and individual levels, so that progress in spelling at different stages of ability may be promoted, and children experiencing difficulties may be detected. Teachers have also been given some information about the origins of our language so that, from a more informed basis, they may make their plans to help (not push) children into becoming confident and enthusiastic writers in an environment which provides both creative and 'real-life' writing experiences.

Bibliography

ADAMS, M. J. (1990) *Beginning to Read*, Cambridge, Massachusetts: MIT Press.

ALBROW, K. (1974) 'The nature of the writing system and its relation to speech, in B. WADE and K. WEDELL (eds.) *Spelling: Task and Learner*, Birmingham University Educational Review: Occasional Publications, no. 5.

BARNES, D. and TODD, F. (1977) *Communication and Learning in Small Groups*, London: Routledge and Kegan Paul.

BBC 2 (1986) *The Story of English* (presented by Robert MacNeil).

BEARD, R. (1984) *Children's Writing in the Primary School*, Sevenoaks, Kent: Hodder and Stoughton.

BEARD, R. (1993) *Teaching Literacy: Balancing Perspectives*, Sevenoaks, Kent: Hodder and Stoughton.

BENNETT, N., DESFORGES, C., COCKBURN, A. and WILKINSON, B. (1984) *The Quality of Pupil Learning Experiences*, Hillsdale, New Jersey, Lawrence Erlbaum Association.

BISSEX, G. (1980) *Gnys at Wrk: A Child Learns to Read and Write*, Cambridge, Massachusetts: Harvard University Press.

BOTHAM, J. (1990) Lecture at Edge Hill College of H.E., *Reading and Writing and the Early Years*.

BRADLEY, H. (1987) *The Making of English* (revised by Simeon Potter), Basingstoke, Hants: Macmillan Education.

BRYANT, P. E. and BRADLEY, L. (1980) 'Why children sometimes write words which they do not read', in U. FRITH (ed.) *Cognitive Processes in Spelling*, London: Academic Press.

BRYANT, P. E. and BRADLEY, L. (1985) *Rhyme and Reason in Reading and Spelling*, University of Michigan Press.

BRADLEY, L. (1990) 'Rhyming connections in learning to read and spell', in P. PUMFREY and C. ELLIOT (eds.) *Children's Difficulties in Reading, Spelling and Writing*, Basingstoke, Hants: Falmer Press.

BRAZIL, D. (1991) Preface to *Collins English Dictionary*, Glasgow: HarperCollins.

BULLOCK, A. (1975) *A Language for Life*, London: H.M.S.O.

BURT, C. (1947) *Mental and Scholastic Tests*, London: Staples.

CARTY, G. (1992) 'Spelling: conversations for change', in *Reading*, vol. 26, no. 2, 17–22, Oxford: Basil Blackwell for U.K.R.A.

CASHDAN, A. (1990) 'Language, communication and reading', in F. POTTER (ed.) *Reading, Learning and Media Education*, Oxford: Blackwell Education.

CATALDO, S. and ELLIS, N. (1990) 'Learning to spell, learning to read, in P. PUMFREY and C. ELLIOT (eds.) *Children's Difficulties in Reading, Spelling and Writing*, Basingstoke, Hants: Falmer Press.

CATO, V., FERNANDES, C., GORMAN, T., KISPAL, A. and WHITE, J. (1992) *The Teaching of Initial Literacy: How Do Teachers Do It?*, Slough, Berks: N.F.E.R.

CHOMSKY, N. and HALLE, M. (1968) *The Sound Pattern of English*, New York: Harper and Row.

CLAY, M. M. (1975) *What Did I Write?*, Auckland, N.Z.: Heinemann.

CLAY, M. M. (1981 reprint) *The Early Detection of Reading Difficulties*, Auckland, N.Z.: Heinemann.

CLAY, M. M. (1990) 'The reading recovery programme, 1984–88: coverage outcomes and education board district figures.' *New Zealand Journal of Educational Studies*, **25**, no. 1, 61–70.

Collins English Dictionary (1991) Glasgow: HarperCollins.

CORNWELL, DR. (1878) *Grammar For Beginners*, London, Edinburgh: Oliver and Boyd.

CRIPPS, C. and PETERS, M. L. (1982) *Appraisal of Current Spelling Materials*, Centre for Teaching of Reading, University of Reading.

CRIPPS, C. and COX, R. (1990) *Joining the ABC. How and Why Handwriting and Spelling Should be Taught Together*, Wisbech, Cambs: L.D.A.

CRYSTAL, D. (1990) *The English Language*, Harmondsworth, Middlesex: Penguin.

CZERNIEWSKA, P. (1989) 'The National Writing Project: thoughts about the early years', in MORAG HUNTER-CARSCH (ed.) *The Art of Reading*, Oxford: Blackwell Education.

DES (1975) *A Language for Life: report of the Committee of Inquiry appointed to the Secretary of State for Education under the chairmanship of Sir Alan Bullock*, London: H.M.S.O.

DES (1978) *Primary Education in England*, London: H.M.S.O.

DES (1982) *Education 5 to 9. An Illustrative Survey of 80 First Schools in England*, London: H.M.S.O.

DES (1984) *English from 5–16. Curriculum Matters 1*, London: H.M.S.O.

DES (June, 1990) *English in the National Curriculum*, London: H.M.S.O.

DES (1992) *Curriculum Organisation and Classroom Practice in Primary Schools*, London: H.M.S.O.

DICKENS, C. (1953, first published 1839) *Nicholas Nickleby*, London: Collins.

DOWNING, J. (1970) 'Relevance versus ritual in learning to read', in *Reading*, **4**, no. 2, 4–12, U.K.R.A.

EHRI, L. C. (1991) 'Learning to read and spell words', in L. RIEBEN and C. A. PERFETTI (eds.) *Learning to Read: Basic Research and its Implications*, Hove, E. Sussex: Lawrence Erlbaum Association.

FOSTER, J. (1991) Lecture at Edge Hill College of Higher Education. *Writing Should be Fun*.

GOODFELLOW, J. (1988) 'Historical background', in R. J. CAMPBELL (ed.) *The Routledge Compendium of Primary Education*, London: Routledge.

GOODMAN, K. S. (1973) *Miscue Analysis*, Illinois: E.R.I.C.

GOSWAMI, U. and BRYANT, P. (1990) *Phonological Skills and Learning to Read*, Hove, E. Sussex: Lawrence Erlbaum Associates.

GRAVES, D. (1983) *Writing: Teachers and Children at Work*, Portsmouth, New Hampshire: Heinemann.

HALL, N. (1987) *The Emergence of Literacy*, Sevenoaks, Kent: Hodder and Stoughton.

HALL, N., MAY, E., MOORES, J., SHEARER, J. and WILLIAMS, S. (1987) 'The literate home corner', in P. SMITH (ed.) *Parents and Teachers Together*, Basingstoke, Hants: Macmillan Education for U.K.R.A.

HALL, N. (1992) 'Play and literacy', in *Language and Literacy News*, no. 8, U.K.R.A.

HANNOVY, S. (1991) 'Middle infant screening test: a safety net for teachers', in *Reading*, **25**, no. 3, 10–15, Oxford: Blackwell for U.K.R.A.

HEATH, S. B. (1983) *Ways with Words: Language Life and Work in Communities and Classrooms*, Cambridge University Press.

HENDERSON, E. and BEERS, J. (1980, eds.) *Developmental and Cognitive Aspects of Learning to Spell*, Newark, Delaware: I.R.A.

HEPBURN, J. (1991) 'Spelling categories and strategies', in *Reading*, **25**, no. 1, 33–7, Oxford: Blackwell for U.K.R.A.

JARMAN, C. (1979) *The Development of Handwriting Skills*, Oxford: Blackwell.

JONES, J. (1988) 'Is that what spelling did to reading?', in *Reading*, **22**, no. 1, 25–31, Oxford: Blackwell for U.K.R.A.

JULEIBO, M. (1985) 'The literacy world of five young children', *Reading – Canada – Lecture*, **3**, no. 2, 126–36.

KINGMAN, J. (1988) *Report of the Committee of Enquiry into the Teaching of English Language*, London: H.M.S.O.

KINNEAVY, J. L. (1971) *A Theory of Discourse*, Englewood Cliffs, New Jersey: Prentice Hall.

LANYON, R. M. (1974) 'An experimental investigation into the relevance of auditory discrimination and articulatory skills for spelling achievement', in WADE and WEDELL (eds.) *Spelling: Task and Learner*, Birmingham University Educational Review: Occasional Publications, no. 5.

LAMBLEY, H. (1992) 'The teaching of reading: the teacher's view?', in *Reading*, **21**, no. 1, Oxford: Basil Blackwell for U.K.R.A.

Letterland ABC (1990), Cambridge: Letterland Ltd.

LITTLEFAIR, A. B. (1989) 'Genre and register: implications for reading', in MORAG HUNTER-CARSCH (ed.) *The Art of Reading*, Oxford: Basil Blackwell for U.K.R.A.

MACKAY, D., THOMPSON, B. and SCHAUB, P. (1970) *Breakthrough to Literacy*, Harlow, Essex: Longman for the Schools Council.

MARSHALL-HUSTON, A. (1991) 'Visual memory: the implications of revisualisation for reading, spelling and writing', in COLIN HARRISON and ERIC ASHWORTH (eds.) *Celebrating Literacy: Defending Literacy*, Oxford: Blackwell for U.K.R.A.

MCGOUGH, R., HENRI, A. and PATTEN, B. (1985) *New Volume*, London: Penguin.

MEEK, M. (1982) *Learning to Read*, London: The Bodley Head.

MICHAEL, I. (1987) *The Teaching of English From the Sixteenth Century to 1870*, Cambridge University Press.

MILLAR, R. and KLEIN, C. (1986) *Making Sense of Spelling*, Inner London Education Authority.

MORRIS, J. M. (1984) 'Phonics 44 for initial literacy in English', in *Reading*, **18**, no. 1, Oxford: Blackwell for U.K.R.A.

MORTIMORE, P., SAMMONS, P., STOLL, L., LEWIS, D. and ECOB, R. (1988) *School Matters: The Junior Years*, Wells, Somerset: Open Books.

MOSELEY, D. (1974) 'Some cognitive and perceptual correlates of spelling ability', in B. WADE and K. WEDDELL (eds.) *Spelling: Task and Learner*, Birmingham University Educational Review: Occasional Publications, no. 5.

MOSELEY, D. and NICOL, C. (1989) *ACE Spelling Dictionary*, Wisbech, Cambs: L.D.A.

MOYLE, D. (1970) *The Teaching of Reading,* London: Wardlock Educational.

MOYLE, D. (1982) *Children's Words*, Oxford: Blackwell.

MUDD, N. (1987) 'I know what you mean . . . I think!', in M. HINSON (ed.) *Support for Learning*, **2**, no. 1, 17–21, Harlow: Longman.

MUDD, N. (1989) 'What Katie did', in *Reading*, **23**, no. 2, Oxford: Blackwell for U.K.R.A.

MUDD, N. (1990a) 'The language of advertising', in FRANK POTTER (ed.) *Reading, Learning and Media Education*, Oxford: Blackwell for U.K.R.A.

MUDD, N. (1990b) *Let's Communicate: A Practical Guide to Adult Basic Education*, Sevenoaks, Kent: Hodder and Stoughton.

National Child Development Study (1983) A.L.B.S.U.

NATIONAL CURRICULUM COUNCIL (1992) *National Curriculum English: The Case for Revising the Order*, Skeldergate, York.

NUNN, SIR T. P. (1930) *Education, Its Date and First Principles*, Arnold and Co.

PERERA, K. (1984) *Children's Writing and Reading: Analysing Classroom Language*, Oxford: Basil Blackwell.

PETERS, M. L. (1970) *Success in Spelling*, Cambridge Institute of Education.

PETERS, M. L. (1975) *Diagnostic and Remedial Spelling Manual*, Basingstoke, Hants: Macmillan Education.

PETERS, M. L. (1985) *Spelling: Caught or Taught? (A New Look)*, London: Routledge and Kegan Paul.

PETERS, M. L. (1987) 'Teaching the catching of spelling', in PETER SMITH (ed.) *Parents and Teachers Together*, Basingstoke, Hants: Macmillan for U.K.R.A.

PETERS, M. L. (1993) 'The teaching of spelling', in ROGER BEARD (ed.) *Teaching Literacy: Balancing Perspectives*, Sevenoaks, Kent: Hodder and Stoughton.

PETERS, M. L. and SMITH, B. (1992) *Spelling in Context: Strategies for Teaching and Learning*, Slough: NFER, Nelson.

POLLOCK, J. (1980) *Signposts to Spelling*, Oxford: Heinemann.

POTTER, S. (1982) *Our Language*, p. 35, Harmondsworth, Middlesex: Penguin.

READ, C. (1986) *Children's Creative Spelling*, London: Routledge and Kegan Paul.

ROBINSON, A. (1988) 'Observations in 5–6 year olds' use of invented spelling', in CHRISTINE ANDERSON (ed.) *Reading: The ABC and Beyond*, Basingstoke, Hants: Macmillan for U.K.R.A.

SASSOON, R. (1990) *Handwriting – The Way to Teach It*, Cheltenham: Stanley Thornes.

SCHONELL, F. J. (1957 reprint) *Essentials in Teaching and Testing Spelling*, Basingstoke, Hants: Macmillan.

SCHONELL, F. J. (1942) *Backwardness in the Basic Subjects*, Edinburgh: Oliver and Boyd.

SCHONELL, F. J. (1985) *Essentials in Teaching and Testing Spelling*, revised by Pamela Wise, Basingstoke, Hants: Macmillan.

SCOTTISH COUNCIL FOR RESEARCH IN EDUCATION (1961) *Studies in Spelling*, University of London Press.

SCRAGG, D. G. (1975) *A History of English Spelling*, Manchester University Press.

SMITH, P. (1977) *Developing Handwriting*, Basingstoke, Hants: Macmillan Education.

STEINBERG, S. H. (1961) *Five Hundred Years of Printing*, Harmondsworth, Middlesex: Penguin.

TEMPLE, C., NATHAN, R., BURRIS, N. and TEMPLE, F. (1993 3rd edn.) *The Beginnings of Writing*, Needham Heights, MA: Allyn and Bacon Inc.

TEMPLETON, S. (1974) 'Spelling, phonology and the older student', in B. WADE and K. WEDELL (eds.) *Spelling: Task and Learner*, Birmingham University Educational Review: Occasional Publications, no. 5.

THORNDIKE, E. L. (1917) 'Reading as reasoning: a study of mistakes in paragraph reading', in *Journal of Educational Psychology*, no. 8, 323–32.

TITLEY, D. P. (1977) *Machines, Money and Men*, Hammersmith, London, HarperCollins: Hart-Davis Educational.

TIZARD, B. and HUGHES, M. (1984) *Young Children Learning: Talking and Thinking at Home and School*, London: Fontana.

TIZARD, B. (1988) 'Literacy developments, *Child Education*, October, p. 11.

TODD, J. (1982) *Learning to Spell: A Book of Resources for Teachers*, Hemel Hempstead, Herts: Simon and Schuster.

TORBE, M. (1979 reprint) *Teaching Spelling*, London: Ward Lock Educational.

TREIMAN, R. (1983) 'The structure of spoken syllables: evidence from novel word games', in *Cognition*, **15**, 49–74.

WADE, B. and WEDELL, K. (1974, eds.) *Spelling: Task and Learner*, Birmingham University Educational Review: Occasional Publications, no. 5.

WALTON, J. (1988) *How Can I Find the Time?*, Reading and Language Development Flyer, Swindon: U.K.R.A.

WATER, M. (1992) Lecture at Edge Hill College of Higher Education, *Reading in the Subject Areas of History and Geography*.

WEDELL, K. (1974) 'A summary of points raised in discussion', in

B. WADE and K. WEDELL (eds.) *Spelling: Task and Learner*, Birmingham University Educational Review: Occasional Publications, no. 5.

WEETABIX (1990) *The Weetabix Wonderword Illustrated Oxford Dictionary*, Oxford University Press.

WRIGHT, J. and CASHDAN, A. (1989) Lecture at Edge Hill College of Higher Education, *Planned Strategies for Readers with Difficulties*.

ZUTELL, J. (1980) 'Children's spelling strategies and their cognitive development', in E. HENDERSON and J. BEERS (eds.) *Developmental and Cognitive Aspects of Learning to Spell*, Newark, Delaware: I.R.A.

Index

p178